"Food addiction is real. It's also ~~discouraging~~ and the endless diets are exhausting and, in most ca_____ Dr. Rhona shares how she won the _____ nd faith together to chart a path to _____
        —Dr. Tim Clinton _____
        Association of Ch_____

"The dilemma in conquering food addiction is that you can't just quit using like an alcoholic or a drug addict. The need to eat exposes us to many triggers that take over our appetites. Dr. Epstein provides a way to put your triggers on safety. If you struggle with weight as I have, you will find something new and very helpful in *Food Triggers*."
        —Stephen Arterburn, author of *Lose It for Life*
        and founder of New Life Ministries

"If you work this plan you will see lasting results! And you don't have to starve yourself. This model is one that can last a lifetime. I highly recommend Dr. Rhona's revolutionary book on how you can achieve results and then maintain consistent results for life!"
        —Thomas Whitman, PhD, founder of
        Life Counseling Services

"Dr. Rhona's unique combination of personal recovery, professional experience, and spiritual power will show you how to create true freedom from addictive eating. Combining scientific truth and overwhelming grace, this book will lead you out of the darkness and help you create your new life."
        —H. Theresa Wright, MS, RD, LDN, Renaissance
        Nutrition Center, Inc., www.sanefood.com

"Anyone who has lost control of their eating and is in search of help will find it here. As a professional who treats addictions, I understand the challenges. *Food Triggers* provides hope for a way to recover."
        —Mark Laaser, PhD, author of *Faithful and True*

"As someone who has struggled most of my life with food, I wish I could have given this book to myself years ago!"
        —Michelle Aguilar, author of *Becoming Fearless* and
        Season 6 winner of *The Biggest Loser*

"A masterpiece of a roadmap designed to bring love, acceptance, freedom, and, most of all, balance back into the lives of those torn up by the claws of addictions."

—Lindsay Roberts, author, speaker, co-host of *The Place for Miracles* and host of *Make Your Day Count*

"If you can't put down the fork, if you never have leftovers, if you're always hungry but never full, if your addiction to food is running your life—buy this book and let it set you free!"

—Daniel G. Amen, MD, author of *Change Your Brain, Change Your Body*

"With scientific truth and overwhelming grace, Dr. Rhona provides escape and a way of rescue for those trapped in the pit of food addiction. Read this book . . . you'll be glad you did!"

—Amy Feigel, licensed professional counselor

"*Food Triggers* offers a new perspective and real answers to those struggling with food addiction. For those who have failed with diet and exercise alone, and felt it was simply a lack of willpower, Rhona Epstein offers hard science and real-life experience to give new hope."

—Jennifer Cisney Ellers, Christian counselor, life coach, and co-author of *The First 48 Hours: Spiritual Caregivers as First Responders*

"Dr. Epstein is one of the few professionals to speak to the tantamount role of spirituality and faith in sustained recovery. . . . I wholeheartedly recommend *Food Triggers* to anyone struggling with the tyranny of addictive eating or dieting."

—Marty Lerner, PhD, CEO, Milestones Eating Disorders Program

"Dr. Rhona has the unique and potent combination of her personal recovery experience as well as professional training to help those still suffering. Her book brings to life what food addiction is, the research that substantiates it, and hope for anyone still suffering. There is a way to freedom!"

—Kim Dennis, MD, CEDS, CEO and medical director, Timberline Knolls

FOOD
TRIGGERS

* END YOUR CRAVINGS *
EAT WELL AND LIVE BETTER

RHONA EPSTEIN, PsyD
— CERTIFIED ADDICTIONS COUNSELOR —

WORTHY®
PUBLISHING

Copyright © 2013 by Rhona Epstein, PsyD, CAC

Published by Worthy Publishing, a division of Worthy Media, Inc., 134 Franklin Road, Suite 200, Brentwood, Tennessee 37027.

Worthy is a registered trademark of Worthy Media, Inc.

HELPING PEOPLE EXPERIENCE THE HEART OF GOD

eBook edition available wherever digital books are sold

Audio distributed through Brilliance Audio; visit brillianceaudio.com

Library of Congress Cataloging-in-Publication Data
Epstein, Rhona.
  Food triggers : end your cravings, eat well, and live better / Rhona Epstein, Psy.D., C.A.C.
    pages cm
  Includes bibliographical references.
  ISBN 978-1-61795-084-1 (trade paper)—ISBN 978-1-61795-158-9
  1. Compulsive eaters. 2. Food habits. 3. Eating disorders. 4. Nutrition. I. Title.
  RC552.C65E7 2013
  616.85'26—dc23

                              2013014708

Many of the names and identifying characteristics of the individuals in this book have been changed to protect their privacy. Some of the individuals described are composites of two or more people.

Because each individual is different and has particular dietary needs or restrictions, the dieting and nutritional information provided in this book does not constitute professional advice and is not a substitute for expert medical advice. Individuals should always check with a doctor before undertaking a dieting, weight loss, or exercise regimen and should continue only under a doctor's supervision. While we provide the advice and information in this book in the hopes of helping individuals lose weight, multiple factors influence a person's weight, and individual results may vary. When a doctor's advice to a particular individual conflicts with advice provided in this book, that individual should always follow the doctor's advice.

All Scripture quotations, unless otherwise indicated, are taken from the New American Standard Bible (NASB). Copyright © 1960, 1962, 1963, 1968, 1971, 1972, 1973, 1975, 1977, 1995 by The Lockman Foundation. Used by permission. Scripture quotations marked NIV are from the Holy Bible, New International Version®. NIV®. Copyright © 1973, 1978, 1984, 2011 by Biblica, Inc. Used by permission. All rights reserved. Scripture quotations marked NLT are from the Holy Bible, New Living Translation, copyright © 1996, 2004, 2007 by Tyndale House Foundation. Used by permission of Tyndale House Publishers, Inc., Carol Stream, Illinois 60188. All rights reserved.

For foreign and subsidiary rights, contact worthypublishing.com

Published in association with Jan Miller of Dupree Miller Associates.

ISBN: 978-1-61795-158-9 (trade paper)

Cover Design: Faceout Studios
Interior Design and Typesetting: Finer Points Productions

Printed in the United States of America
13 14 15 16 17 VP 8 7 6 5 4 3 2 1

For all of my dear clients,
who have opened themselves to change,
and all those now enjoying freedom,
and those still in the battle:
we can live freely.

CONTENTS

PART THREE
Beating Your Triggers: A Plan

You Can Stop the Triggers

You were just going to take a taste, but one bite led to more and ended in a pile of leftover wrappers, packages, sacks, and containers. Or you love someone who's living this way. You aren't sure how that first mouthful led to the consumption of an unmentionable amount of something-something, but you don't want to talk about it. You couldn't bear for anyone to know about the gluttony, even though the evidence is right there in the pounds piling on. Whatever you call it—pigging out, bingeing, abusing food, getting a food fix— you pray no one knows about the shameful indulgence as you try to hide the evidence.

The fact is this secret life is not so secret anymore.

It's epidemic.

Any given month in America, between six and fifteen million people binge out of control, according to the National Institute of Mental Health.[1] Yet nowhere near this many people ever get help. Millions of overeaters never get treatment. Meanwhile, food manufacturers keep introducing newfangled processed foods designed to be irresistible in taste and texture, with synthetic flavor enhancers. Think about how many new potato chip, soft drink, cookie, cracker, and ice cream flavors or brands you've been introduced to in advertisement blitzes in the last month alone.

At risk are people who spend their days and nights obsessing about food and consuming it in voluminous amounts. Or those who don't necessarily obsess but who find themselves in situations that spiral out of control. Or those who go into debt or spend their last dollars on a carton and container for a fix one day and a new diet plan or program and exercise equipment or regimen the next.

You may be one of those people.

You may be someone who knows and loves one of those people.

Either way, a life is being eaten away. Food is costing something: health, money, relationships, vocation, hobbies, peace.

That's why I wrote this book—because life can be better. You or your loved one can be free from a mad cycle with food. You can eat in healthy ways and focus on things that matter more than a cookie or a chip, a slice of cheesecake or a sliver of pie.

I want you to know there's a reason people pig out, overeat, and find themselves addicted to foods or snacks consumed in an outrageous amount in a single sitting. Contrary to myth, it's not because of being fat and stupid, lazy and indulgent and greedy, or having no willpower or pride. In fact, it takes a lot of work, creativity, and intelligence to hide overeating and binges, food abuse and addiction, from a world that frowns on overweight bodies and links overeating to obesity.

Every day another diet book will tell you the person who overeats just needs to exercise more self-control—or exercise, period—or substitute carrot sticks and celery for cookies and ice cream—or eat in moderation. Every day another program or person will try to convince you life will be better when you're skinny. Such advice couldn't be more disastrous for the person whose brain is hardwired to be triggered by certain foods or who falls prey to foods designed to be addictive. Diets and exercise programs are not remotely the whole answer for how to stop the madness that goes on with overeating, whether on occasion or repeatedly to the point of ruining your life.

There's a bigger picture. And help for you or someone you love hiding the empties, piling on the pounds, obsessing over food (even now and then), and riding the roller coaster of eating and overeating. The basic truths we'll look at together in this book are:

- Chemical properties of certain foods, coupled with faulty brain wiring, can contribute to overeating.

- You can determine whether you have a trigger issue that is controlled by avoiding certain foods, or if you have an addiction to those foods and need a course for recovery.
- There are ways to eat that allow you to make peace with food and yourself, lose weight, and find wholeness.

In the chapters that follow, you'll find the science on what's causing this epidemic of overeating and the research on what happens in the body and brain when certain foods trigger the urge to binge. You'll also see practical help on what you can do about it (whether you're the overeater or you love one), hope and encouragement for a better life, and motivation in the true stories of people who are overcoming lives of overeating.

Food doesn't have to cost you your life, dollars, relationships, and dreams—or your passion for a full and abundant way of living.

Many doctors, counselors, scientists, researchers, and therapists are now focusing on this epidemic. They're asking questions like whether the issues are biological or psychological, and if the root of the problem is in the behavior of overeating or hard wiring in the brain to overeat and addiction. They're working to understand why eating, something essential to life, as needed and natural as air and shelter or sleep, must sometimes be treated or managed.

The good news is they're finding answers. There is help.

Recently, I met with a new client about her food struggles, and she said it took her years to get to my office. She tried for most of her life to hide her binges. She's a highly intelligent and successful woman who said she couldn't believe she had gotten to a place where she needed to pay a therapist to talk about food. She was so ashamed she put her face in her hands and began to cry, embarrassed, wanting to hide all over again.

I was moved because I knew what it was like to sit in that chair, my face in my hands in shame. I understood wanting the struggle to disappear, along with the weight and the burden of continuing to lose control.

"You're not alone," I shared, "and you're not beyond help. What if you knew there was a chemical explanation? What if this insanity was a treatable illness? Wouldn't that make a difference in how you felt and approached recovery?"

Immediately my client's tears stopped. She looked up, stunned. She then straightened in her chair, taller, brighter, lighter. It was as if a leaden shawl had been lifted from her shoulders and then her mind and then her very soul. I could almost see my words running through her mind: *Chemical explanation. Treatable. Recovery.*

There *is* a chemical explanation for the binges and overeating patterns. Losing control to a food trigger and food addiction are treatable. You, or the one you love who overeats, can live free.

One thing I know for sure: we are not alone, and God never meant for us to live in agony over what was created to nurture and sustain us. He never meant for us to struggle with food.

So believe that you can end the cycle. Have faith in what your or your loved one's future can be.

I know because I've broken free from the bondage of addictive eating.

You can too.

♡ Rhona

My Story

He brought me up out of the pit of destruction,
out of the miry clay, and He set my feet
upon a rock making my footsteps firm.
—PSALM 40:2

G rowing up, sugar was my drug of choice. It was like heroin for me. Like most children my age, I enjoyed candy and cookies for dessert, but my seemingly normal affection for sugary treats led to an intense and raging battle that eventually brought me to a very bad place. I was only a teenager, but I wanted to die.

When I ate sweets, I couldn't stop. I routinely ate until I became ill. Like a junkie, I craved sugar and I was willing to do about anything to get it: lie to my family and friends, avoid social situations, hide food wrappers, whatever it took to binge in secret. It wasn't unusual to eat a half gallon of ice cream, a box of cookies, a jar of peanut butter, and a bag of chips all in one sitting.

This was all done in isolation, of course. No one could ever know so I had to become a master at hiding the evidence. I remember taking frozen bagels from the freezer and trying desperately to defrost them without using a microwave or oven to avoid making noise in the kitchen. I used to attempt to hide my ice cream binges by trying to make the top of the ice cream in the container look exactly like it did before I dug into it. Over and over, I would fix the top until the whole container was empty. Then I'd rush to the store to buy a new container of ice cream and make it look like the one before. I had special hiding places for my candy wrappers, places I kept them until just the right time to discard them without anyone knowing.

I threw away food and swore I was done with it, only to go back later, pull it out of the trash, and eat what remained. Swearing I'd never binge again became my daily mantra. Promises to quit were quickly broken by failures to follow through. A moment of weakness would cripple me, and I'd find myself eating an entire dozen doughnuts on my thirty-minute ride home.

I lived in fear of being caught. The pain was intense. I was completely out of control and hopeless.

Exercise was another part of the insanity. I spent hours every day running, swimming, or doing sit-ups, attempting to repair the damage done by my extensive overeating. Of course, it was impossible to rid myself of all of the calories I was consuming during my binges. When exercise didn't seem like enough, I wore a sweat suit and sat in a sauna, hoping to sweat off the fat. I figured losing water weight was better than losing no weight at all.

Every attempt at change failed. Diets were short-lived. I tried WeightWatchers, the Scarsdale diet, the Pritikin diet, diet pills, appetite suppressants, fasting, purging, Fit for Life, overnight camp for overweight teens, and weight loss diet bars. Each new plan brought new hope, but that hope was short-lived too. My self-esteem was destroyed from constantly failing to change, and after years of binges I had an overweight body that just added to my desperation.

> I was trapped in a world where sugar controlled me, and I was losing everything in my life except the weight.

Every area of my life was impacted. I couldn't concentrate in school because I was constantly thinking about food, dieting, or concealing the fat rolls under my baggy clothes. Ashamed and embarrassed by my weight, I avoided social situations and opted for isolation so I could better keep my secret. I lost friends, and my family relationships became strained. I was angry that nobody understood me, and I was angry when anyone interfered or commented on anything relating to food or my body size.

I was trapped in a world where sugar controlled me, and I was losing everything in my life except the weight.

Part of the trap was the silence. Back in the late 1970s and early 1980s, eating disorders were a mystery. They were rarely talked about in the media, and most people didn't know anything about binge-eating disorder, bulimia, or anorexia. No one knew how much pain I was in because I worked hard to keep a happy exterior. Happy on the outside, dying on the inside. To most people, I looked like a normal teen having a good time. In reality, I was trapped inside a living hell. Every day I wished I were dead.

I saw a counselor a few times. As I poured out my heart to her, telling her about the battle I'd been hiding from the world, she looked puzzled. She diagnosed me as "depressed" and sent me on my way.

She was right. I was depressed, but that was just a symptom of a much deeper problem. I was a seventeen-year-old mess who needed a miracle. That's exactly what I found when I least expected it.

I was visiting another diet organization to try yet another diet plan in hopes of resolving my weight problem. I wanted to ask my parents for more money to pay for this new miracle cure, but a deep sense of guilt overwhelmed me. *Who was I kidding?* I thought. *I can spend my parents' money and bring home all of the prepackaged diet food, and there's still no chance I'll actually follow the plan.*

For the first time, I got real with myself. I'd spent much of my life acting like I was following a diet in front of everyone, while in secret I consumed enough food for ten people. I just couldn't play the game anymore. I walked away from that diet center and into a support group for overeaters. I didn't know it then, but this was my first step toward recovery. I found out I wasn't alone. A lot of others had done the same insane things with food that I had. A lot of others had learned how to stop.

This was a revelation and the glimmer of possibility I needed.

There was hope for someone like me.

But the road from hope to recovery was just beginning.

The early days of recovery were all about opening up and

receiving help. I was so used to keeping things secret that being transparent and honest was a new concept. Over time, I felt less ashamed talking about my out-of-control binges and secret eating because the people in the group had all done the same thing. They truly understood. I also learned recovery was more than simply dropping the unwanted pounds that had resulted from my binge eating. To experience true freedom, I'd have to make physical, emotional, and spiritual changes.

> **I had to face the fact that just one bite of a sugary food was too much, and a thousand bites would never be enough. Like an alcoholic, I could never have just a little.**

Physically, I had to come to terms with my addiction to certain foods—mainly sugar. I had to face the fact that just one bite of a sugary food was too much, and a thousand bites would never be enough. Like an alcoholic, I could never have just a little. And, I had to make serious changes in the way I related to food. I needed a structured eating plan that included all of the healthy foods necessary to keep my body going. Diets were no longer okay. I needed balanced meals without restricting or compensating for excessive eating later. No purging, starving, or bingeing. I tried different levels of rigidity with food until I found a plan I could live with. While some in my support group needed to be very strict about every morsel they ate, that didn't work for me. I needed a looser structure. I needed boundaries with some flexibility. Through trial and error, I found a plan that put food in its proper place. Physically, I was getting better. The weight was coming off.

Emotionally, however, I had a lot of work to do. I had numbed my feelings for so long that I was relatively unaware of what was going on inside. I used different vehicles to help uncover the reason I felt compelled to eat. I tried journaling and reading about feelings so I could understand more about myself. I found that I had anger, bitterness, fear, insecurity, pride, and sadness stored up inside of me. I learned that I was a highly sensitive person who was really good at hiding my true self. I had never known what to do with my intense emotions, so I ate.

To find true freedom, I had to change my whole way of thinking. Instead of shoving all of my feelings deep inside, I learned to deal with them one at a time. I also had to accept that some things simply couldn't be changed or fixed, and that was okay.

It became very clear that in order to truly recover, I would have to keep my soul clean. I couldn't let anger or fear build inside of me. I had to see emotions gone wild for what they were—a setup for overeating. I had to learn how to choose peace again and again.

Of all the gifts of recovery, the greatest gift was finding God. I was raised in a Jewish home, but our practices were more cultural than spiritual. God was not a part of anything personal to me. He was something connected to religion, nature, others—not me. But a woman I trusted, also in recovery, told me I would never get free physically or emotionally without coming to know God personally.

So I started out saying a few simple prayers and meditating on a few Bible verses. This went on for years until the truth of God's promises of love, freedom, and strength began to sink in. I discovered my ability to be free was totally dependent on Him. I would never have enough willpower to do this on my own. (Food addiction is not about willpower anyway.) All of my attempts to change had failed miserably. But relying on God and His strength instead of myself brought about true metamorphosis.

This spiritual journey has been wonderful, but it hasn't been easy. It's been, as the Bible calls it, "the good fight of faith" (1 Timothy 6:12). But it has become a lifestyle that goes way beyond food addiction. Walking with God changed everything. Instead of living in isolation and fear, I now live in fellowship and faith. God has enabled me to grow in ways I couldn't have imagined possible. Looking back, I can honestly say my greatest challenges have been what led me to the greatest blessings of my life.

Eventually I went back to see the psychologist who had diagnosed me with depression, and she looked even more confused than the first time I'd seen her, as I shared my story of freedom from food addiction. I'm certain she didn't realize my food abuse had been an addiction, and depression was a secondary diagnosis that disappeared with the resolution of the food addiction. Even as I told her about overcoming my struggles with secretive eating and bingeing, she didn't seem to understand.

She's not alone.

Most people do not understand food addiction. We live in a culture where loss of control with food is fairly common, where people even make light of it. How many skits on *Saturday Night Live* or movies have you seen where someone downs their troubles in pints of ice cream and piles of candy bars? How often is the overweight actor shown going crazy, and going for laughs, in a binge scene?

This transfers to real life. How often do the people around you gorge on cookie dough and pizza on Sunday night and simply go on a little diet to get back on track Monday morning? How many of them try to make light of it, just like the actors we see on TV? These folks can't imagine losing control to the point of having their lives destroyed. But it happens.

It happened to me. It's happened to countless others. It happens to someone every day. It may be happening to you right now.

If you're not yet on the road to recovery from food addiction or some other eating disorder, this book is a step in the right direction. Not only have I spent my life earning degrees in counseling and helping thousands of people just like you over the past twenty-eight years, but I can say I've been there. I know what you're going through. I know the shame and guilt you wake up with every morning and go to bed with every night. I know how many times you've tried to lose weight, only to blow a diet and gain it all, maybe more, back. I know how discouraged and hopeless and lonely it feels.

I know something else too.

I know how to get free. I know how to stay free. Now I'm going to show you how.

PART ONE

The Science of Triggers

I don't really understand myself, for I want to do what is right, but I don't do it. Instead, I do what I hate. But if I know that what I am doing is wrong, this shows that I agree [with what's] good. . . . I want to do what is right, but I can't. I want to do what is good, but I don't. I don't want to do what is wrong, but I do it anyway. . . . I have discovered this principle of life—that when I want to do what is right, I inevitably do what is wrong. . . . There is another power within me that is at war with my mind. This power makes me a slave. . . . Oh, what a miserable person I am! Who will free me from this life?

—ROMANS 7:15–24 (NLT)

ONE

Willpower or Wiring?

L ast night I had an out-of-control binge. I ate everything I could get my hands on: a tub of Ben & Jerry's ice cream, the new bag of Doritos in the cabinet, and then the chocolate chip cookies. I ate until I was sick.

But it's okay. I know today will be different. I'll never do that again. Today I'll start my new diet. I'll lose the twenty, thirty, seventy pounds I've wanted to lose forever. I have a plan. I can already see myself in my thinner body, wearing cute clothes, feeling confident in my own skin.

So here I go. Breakfast. Hey, this isn't so bad. I'm doing okay. I feel good.

Afternoon. What a day! I'm hungry. Maybe I'll just have a snack, not a cookie, but these crackers. Maybe just a handful. Only it's not very much. I'm still hungry. Maybe just one more handful . . .

Wow. I didn't mean to eat the whole box. The snack I didn't plan on has turned, once again, into a binge. I've blown the diet. I might as well go for what I really want and start over tomorrow. But I don't want anyone to see me sneaking into the fridge. Maybe if I just get some more peanut butter from the cupboard. Oh, and these cookies.

Now I've done it. Really done it. I can barely move. I've blown it again. How could I? What just happened anyway? Didn't I say I was going to stick to my diet? Didn't I start well this morning? I was so determined, so sure today would be different. Why can't I get a grip? Why do I think of food and eating all day? Why am I so anxious about eating . . . and not eating, and if I can eat a lot, or there will only be a little to eat?

And look at me! No, I can't look. How can anyone stand me? People *must wonder why I've let myself go. No matter how much I hide and sneak, they must know. The fact that I binge is all over me. It's so distracting too. How can I concentrate on my work? My family isn't getting what they need. I'm doing the best I can, but my best seems to just barely get me through the day. My best just isn't good enough.*

I'm not good enough.

What's wrong with me? I hate myself. There was a brief time I looked good. Why couldn't I stay that way? Why did I keep eating? How did I get back here, to this weight? I've gained back almost all of what I'd lost.

Lord, help me. I don't know why I'm such a mess, why I'm never satisfied. I always feel fat and can't stop eating. Who can understand such craziness? I've tried a thousand different diets. Low fat. Low carb. Only fruits and vegetables. WeightWatchers. Jenny Craig. Protein diets. Diet pills. Diet foods. Diets that starve me. Purging. Nothing works. I'm tired of following all these things. Why do I end up losing control again?

I'm such a failure.

THE SCRIPT OF OUR LIVES

Sound familiar? How often have you returned to this script? Over and over? Once in a while? Have you made any of these same promises to yourself, only to fail miserably? Have you on occasion—not every day, but enough—lost control like my friend Ginger, who wasn't a food addict but couldn't seem to stop eating chocolate chip cookies, so she binged on Saturday but restarted her diet on Sunday?

You're not alone.

Most of us are bombarded by what we describe as "weight" problems with diets. We keep looking for the perfect solution. We try exercise plans and pills that promise a weight loss miracle. Some people go as far as to get liposuction and bariatric surgery. Ultimately, our efforts and these things fail. We're painfully disappointed in ourselves when we go off the diet plan after only a few days—or even worse, lose a lot of weight then regain it all and more. When will-power fails repeatedly, even though our desire to change is strong, we wonder if something is hindering our ability to gain control.

Something deeper *is* at work. That something calls for us to change the way we think about our weight. It means it's time to stop worrying so much about the numbers on the scale and start examining the deeper issues.

A dysfunctional relationship with food.

Food abuse and addiction.

Overeating and eating disorders.

Chemistry of the brain and body.

All four are behind that familiar script—different names or terms for the same problem are on the rise.[1] Obesity has become a pressing, worldwide health concern. In fact, obesity is now the second leading preventable cause of death in the United States.[2]

But here's the important connection: a lot of people think they are overweight because of a lack of self-control. That can be true, but something else is probably at work too, something unknown to science and consumers until just a few years ago. That something operates beyond the strength of willpower and it's as deadly to your body as to the mind and spirit. Yet you're made to feel as though it's your fault, which is as criminal as if you went to the doctor for a check-up and the physician tapped the spot right below your knee that made your leg jerk and then snapped, "Stop that! If you only had more willpower, you could keep your knee from jerking! Shame on you!"

Wouldn't it be unfair? Isn't it abusive?

That's exactly the case with many people fighting weight with diets. The cause of the problem is their brains hardwired a certain way, not their willpower (or lack of it). People keep beating themselves up for being failures and not having more resolve when there's quite possibly a chemical reason they struggle with not just weight but killer eating disorders, binges, and food addictions.

You might be one of those people. The way your brain works may be what has kept you from stopping the triggers to overeating and weight gain. Chemistry may be what makes you eat as you do and makes you miserable not just on the outside but deep within.

What if, instead of snapping, "Shame on you," your doctor told you how understanding that chemistry can change your relationship with food forever?

What if it could change your life?

Well, a doctor *is* telling you. I'm telling you what you're about to learn can change your life—for good.

THE WEIGHT OF FOOD TRIGGERS

There is indeed a physiological process, a chemistry in the brain that—along with emotional, environmental, and spiritual issues— can keep even the most diligent dieter from succeeding. You can be addicted to food, just as the alcoholic is to liquor. There is substantial evidence some people lose control over food consumption, cannot reduce their intake, cannot quit eating certain types of food, and cannot reduce the amount they eat even when faced with negative consequences.

Chemical reactions can take over the brain, just as with substance abuse, making it difficult for certain people to refrain from overeating.

Have you been there? You decide to allow yourself one chocolate chip cookie, and before you know it you've eaten all the cookies in the jar. Is it simply a lack of willpower or is something deeper going on, something physical driving that cookie binge? Well, according to the latest food abuse research, chemical reactions can take over the brain, just as with substance abuse, making it difficult for certain people to refrain from overeating.

For example, take ghrelin and leptin, the technical names for two hormones little-known to most of us. I simply call them *hungry* and *full*. You may not have known those hormones' names but you know how they make you feel. When they're operating optimally, they work together to make you feel hungry or full. The *hungry* levels rise when your body thinks you need food, and *full* levels rise when you've eaten enough and should feel satisfied. And when these hormones aren't working right? They can trigger you to eat . . . and eat and eat.

Here's the problem: People who have low levels of the *full* hormone never get the signal to feel full, which makes them continue eating. When these people persist in overeating, the brain becomes dulled and unresponsive to the *full* hormone. Their appetites never shut down as they should. It may not be that they don't have enough willpower to resist the second, third, and fourth helping. It may be

TRIGGER TALK

The Power of Knowing and Believing

When you love someone who has struggled with food, you see how powerless they (and you) can feel. What's the answer? Where's the key? If only you both knew.

Now someone you love is beginning to understand why they're bingeing—and the truth can feel overwhelming. You can help them see that they can overcome. Remind the person struggling (even if it means printing this on a card to keep handy):

- **You are not a freak.** You're someone who's abused food.
- **You're not alone.** You're among thousands of others.
- **You're not rewarding yourself with snacks that are snares.** You're rewiring yourself for freedom that's transforming.
- **God's behind that kind of power.** "Do not be discouraged," He says (Joshua 1:9 NIV). In encouragement you'll find His strength, His promise to go with you on this journey "wherever you go."

their *full* hormone is non-operational, so what starts out as a normal meal turns into an all-out binge.

It gets worse. Some people with severe food problems can be triggered to binge simply by looking at pictures of certain types of foods.[3] These people's brains show they experience actual biochemical cravings just from seeing the pictures.

Advertisers have been banking on this idea since long before it was ever proven. It's why billboards feature juicy cheeseburgers with the words NEXT EXIT. Think about it: The mere image of a cheeseburger can actually lure some motorists from a predetermined route and schedule.

Why doesn't this work with every motorist? Why can the picture of a juicy burger consume some people with a quest to find and eat that food while others can glance at the ad and go merrily on their way? Is it simply that some people are readily influenced and others are like Teflon?

Not at all. Neuroscientists are finding certain individuals appear to have brain wiring that makes them more sensitive to food signals.[4] Researchers use the term "external food sensitivity" (EFS) to describe people who have cravings after smelling or seeing food, even when they aren't hungry. It seems subjects with high EFS have different wiring in the regions of the brain related to eating (the amygdala and the ventral striatums). The timing of signals in these brain regions is slightly off in people with high EFS.

You may be chemically prone to food addiction.

It means that if your brain is wired a certain way, you may be chemically prone to food addiction.

Did you catch that? You're not crazy. You're not beyond hope or help. There's a reason for what you do, and you can overcome it.

TWO

The Chemistry of Triggering

Does it sound outlandish that you could be addicted to food, something we're made to need for survival?

It shouldn't. Food addicts and drug and alcohol addicts have so much in common: loss of control; cravings; denial of the extent of problems; preoccupation; the use of food or substances to cope with stress; secretiveness; negative effects in relationships; and social, psychological, and occupational consequences.

Food addicts and drug and alcohol addicts share something else too—the same kind of brain chemistry:[1]

- **Personality profiles are similar** in individuals who binge-eat and who are cocaine addicts.
- **Bulimic clients have higher addictiveness scores** than people with anorexia or people with normal eating patterns.
- **People with eating disorders, particularly bulimia, show behavior patterns of multiple addictions.** For instance, female bulimics have been found to have alcohol and drug addictions too.
- **Individuals use alcohol and food as substitutes for each other**, often using one to avoid the other and vice versa.
- **Clients admit starving or bingeing can enhance their drugs' euphoric effects**.
- **Addicts may use drugs to decrease eating**, and conversely, they may use eating to avoid drug abuse.

- **Heroin and alcohol addicts show a heightened preference for sweets** and often experience sweet cravings.
- **Some alcoholics eat candy to help avoid alcohol**, and may become addicted to sweets and refined carbohydrates.

Those last two similarities between the addict of food and the alcoholic and drug addict are especially striking. Addicts prefer sweets, experience cravings for sweets, and become as addicted to them as their go-to substances.

Sugar Is a Trigger

Science is confirming that. Professor Bart Hoebel and his colleagues at Princeton University's Neuroscience Institute found sugar does have long-lasting effects in the brain of a sugar addict just as alcohol has in the brain of an alcoholic and drugs in the brain of a drug addict.

"Craving and relapse are critical components of addiction," Hoebel said, "and we have been able to demonstrate these behaviors in sugar-bingeing rats in a number of ways."[2]

First, his sugar-loving rats experienced the same neurochemical changes in the brain as those produced by addictive drugs such as cocaine, morphine, and nicotine. When the rats drank a sugary solution, the feel-good chemical dopamine was released in their brains, signaling motivation, repetition, and addiction. Indeed, after a month of sugar-bingeing, the structure of the rats' brains actually changed; they had fewer feel-good, satisfied dopamine receptors and more opioid receptors, which are the parts of the brain that seek motivation and reward. This was similar to the brain changes in rats hooked on cocaine and heroin.

You may not be a rat, but if you're hardwired this way, your brain would go through the same changes, whether you were hooked on sugar or cocaine. It means you'd also go through the same things in reverse, too, just as the rats did. When researchers took away their sugar, the rats showed signs of withdrawal, just like people who are kicking the habit. The feel-good chemicals in the brain went way down. Fear and anxiousness increased to the extent that their teeth chattered and they lacked confidence to explore their surroundings. They cowered in their habitats in hope of finding more of the sugary soda on which they'd become hooked.

Sugar, after all, was their drug of choice.

Another study with rats and sugar revealed something even more troubling: rats allowed to binge on foods rich in sugar and fat for a two-month period became so addicted that when healthier foods were presented to them two months later, they chose to go hungry before eating anything but the sugar and fat they craved.[3]

Did you get that? The rats would *starve* themselves rather than free themselves from the high they got on sugar and fat.

In a way, the same thing happens with people. Think how much junk food, made up mostly of sugar and fat or both, debilitates us. Sugar and fat can actually desensitize the reward pathway in our brains so we need more and more in

> **Sugar and fat can actually desensitize the reward pathway in our brains so we need more and more in order to experience the same happy feeling as before.**

order to experience the same happy feeling as before. Nothing else, including healthy foods, satisfies, not for the rats, nor for the food and sugar addict.

You may understand that all too well. Yesterday, it may have only taken one candy bar to boost your mood. Today, you might need two candy bars to bring back the happy. It is a rat race, isn't it, experiencing a true chemically driven craving?

Chemistry Is a Cause

What makes you a true hardwired food addict? What makes you someone who, because of your body chemistry, is more likely to become easily addicted to certain food ingredients?

The answer can take careful exploration. To start, look at the chemical reaction that goes on in the brain of the hardwired food addict:

- You feel more pain, become angry or depressed more easily, and experience a kind of panic that drives you to want to eat sugar in order to feel better, all because you have deficits of serotonin, the chemical in your brain that controls these feelings.
- Your hunger feels satisfied less often and you crave more of a substance or food, because you have fewer of those feel-good dopamine receptors.
- You find it seemingly impossible to have a healthy, balanced relationship with food (meaning no overeating and binges) because of imbalances in the release of endorphins and enkephalins (maybe all at the same time).

The problem is you can never eat enough sugar to feel how you want to feel. Each binge sets in motion an uncontrollable chemical process that has a feedback loop. Like a hamster on a wheel, you want to eat even more sugar. It's a vicious circle: eating refined carbohydrates stimulates the pancreas to release insulin, which decreases the concentration of amino acids, which manufacture serotonin in the bloodstream, which causes a drop in blood sugar level, which results in feelings of weakness and hunger and headaches and trembling. Every drop in blood sugar for the food addict triggers a person to eat more refined carbohydrates to offset the symptoms, and round and round it goes.

Sound exhausting?

It gets worse. Such food cravings trigger reinforcing chemicals: the "endogenous opiate" manufactured by your own body to numb you, creating effects similar to taking morphine.[4] Whenever you ingest sweet or other palatable foods, you can get these pain-killing effects. The result is like that old song says, "If loving you is wrong, I don't want to be right." You feel too good eating sugary foods and experiencing the rush of those good-mood chemicals to give them up. Instead, you live from one sugar high to the next, never wanting to lose that sugar buzz, and here's why.

Trauma and Anxiety Bring It On—Low Serotonin

While the reasons aren't exactly clear why some people have this wiring problem in the brain and others don't, clues suggest you can be genetically predisposed. Just as babies carried by a drug-abusing mom can start life with an addiction, you can also be affected in the womb by anxiety and trauma, which trigger the faulty hard wiring.

For example, a mother is abused or suffers an addiction herself that leads to out-of-control and at-risk behaviors like physical blackouts and falls, fights, and feuds. The anxiety affects the brain chemistry, actually changing the serotonin system. Because trauma and anxiety go hand in hand, additional trauma results. The child carried by the mom faces anxiousness, which can cause more childhood trauma, which when faced as an adult brings on more anxiety, and so forth. A setup for food addiction or other types of problems.

Anxiety caused by other situations in life can trigger faulty hard wiring in the brain too. Constant fear, for example, can create too much adrenaline flow, and since you're already lacking serotonin and other brain-calming chemicals, the rush from adrenaline and the lack of calming chemicals creates confusion. Have you had too much? Too little? Are you hungry? Full? Your brain signals your body to search for an answer that might lie in a food craving.

Anxiety triggers can come from other things too: a dramatic episode or series of traumas over a long period of time or even day-to-day, low-level, chronic stress such as daily tiffs with your husband or kids or problems with the boss at work.

Well-Being Is Inhibited—Low Dopamine Receptors

Another type of faulty wiring appears to be that some brains may not have as many dopamine receptors as other brains. Remember, dopamine is that feel-good chemical that stress (good or bad) can release. Dopamine helps you cope by giving you a sense of well-being. It can ease your stress, put you in the mood for love, and give you happiness about eating. To work correctly, though, you have to have enough dopamine receptors. Compare it to airplanes needing runways to land. If you're hardwired so you don't have enough runways for the feel-good dopamine to land, you won't feel as good as you should, no matter how much of the chemical your brain makes. It means you might eat a half gallon of ice cream trying to get more feel-good dopamine. But you already lack enough feel-less-pain serotonin so

TRIGGER TALK

Telling Your Trigger

So you're awakened to how important it is to worry less about weight and more about the real problem, how your relationship with foods triggers the hard wiring in your brain to eat without stopping. Just what is the relationship anyway? What triggers you?

Go where you won't be interrupted or distracted and answer in writing:

- What is my first memory of craving, wanting, needing a particular thing to eat?
- What food was it?
- Where was I? What was the situation?
- How old was I? How did I feel about myself?
- How did I feel while eating? Immediately after? A few hours later? The next day?

Now write down your next memory of a craving, and a third memory, answering the questions above for each memory.

What patterns do you see? Is there clearly one food or type of food that triggers episodes of overeating?

Hang on to this and add to it, writing down more memories about your relationship with food. Each time you do, you take another step toward recovery: identifying trigger foods, looking for patterns, finding where you can stop the binges and start living more fully.

your brain says, "keep eating the ice cream" with hope more sero-tonin will lead to more feel-good dopamine. Instead, you can eat ten gallons of ice cream and nothing much happens other than you gain weight and activate the damaging cycle: gaining weight makes you feel worse in all sorts of ways, which makes you want to eat more and more sugar.

This is what can cause you to consume large amounts of sugar in the same way cocaine addicts take drugs. It's the same chemicals, working in the same way. Cocaine addicts are trying to feel better, but they can't because they don't have any dopamine runways either.

Think about it. Maybe you're not eating ice cream every night. But what about when you're stressed about a presentation that went badly at work? Or when your spouse begins to work late and it feels like he or she is never available. Or when you're feeling overwhelmed with the kids this week. You want to feel better, and desserts do the trick—at least, for a while, until the next time you feel bad and eat the whole package of mini-doughnuts in one sitting, which makes you feel worse . . . and . . . See how the cycle continues?

What a painful scenario to experience and witness.

To add insult to this injury, people with higher body mass also have fewer dopamine receptors than people with lower body mass.[5] If your brain is already hardwired for food addiction and you're obese too (situations can literally feed on one another), then you have two strikes against you. Dopamine deficiencies in the obese actually can promote and sustain out-of-control eating because dopamine helps food stimulate the reward centers of the brain.

This is a vivid picture of how the cards can be stacked against you if you're a food addict, without you ever knowing. It also brings to light the subtle undercurrent of why hardwired people may actu-ally realize they're killing themselves with food, but continue eating anyway: Taking risks sets off a chain reaction of chemicals in the brain that leads to more "I feel good" dopamine being released. The more people with this hard wiring harm themselves, the more they actually feel better.

Feelin' Groovy Becomes a Need—
High Beta-Endorphins and Low Enkephalins

The way one feels is exactly what frames food addiction. Compulsive overeaters have been found to have higher levels of beta-endorphins, a type of opiate the body produces to lower pain and make you feel better. So when the food addict eats and the brain releases feel-good chemicals, those higher beta-endorphins signal "keep eating, this feels good."

By the same token, overeaters also have lower levels of certain enkephalins, another morphinelike, painkilling substance. If you need to eat a lot to keep the chemicals at a certain minimum level and feel all right, then you eat even more. This explains why people prone to food addiction crave refined carbohydrates. Eating only a few grams of refined carbs can create a better mood by bringing their brain chemistry into balance, so they keep going back for another powdered doughnut.

What I find most interesting is that food addicts, like drug and alcohol addicts, are hardwired to try to reproduce the natural substances their brains are not producing. So they eat, just as the alcoholic takes another drink, to keep at bay the withdrawal symptoms:

- Sluggishness
- Headaches
- Irritability
- Rapidly changing mood swings
- Sleep disturbance
- Sadness
- Anger
- Anxiety
- Cravings

No wonder withdrawal for the food addict can be painful in a physical way as these withdrawal symptoms (and more) are for the drug addict. No wonder then there is a physical urge to keep eating because of the hard wiring to feel good. No wonder the hard wiring distinction is important to understand in order to ever kick the overeating habit.

THREE

Know Thyself

There's an old proverb that there is no shame in not knowing—the shame is in not finding out. So when you hear the term "food addict," do you think, *That's not me*? Maybe you're just trigger sensitive instead? Wouldn't it be a shame not to know?

Nancy, fifty-three, told me how every time she tried to cut out eating sugar and refined carbohydrates like white bread, she experienced symptoms that mimicked withdrawal from addictive drugs. I asked if she'd ever heard of food addiction.

She hadn't, but even as we began to look into it, she was sure she was addicted to sugar. By midlife she had been on a dieting roller coaster more years than not. The ups and downs with food started in her preteen years, when she first became and stayed overweight. She could lose weight, but like so many food addicts, she couldn't seem to keep it off. She would always go back to overeating and binges on desserts. She read every new diet book, tried every possible means to control her weight, and always ended up heavier than the time before.

She wanted to know how to eat well and be fit. So I suggested a different approach. She started a structured plan of eating, stopped overindulging in the sugar and refined carbohydrates, and began attending 12-step meetings to address addictive issues.

Once again, almost immediately, she struggled with the withdrawal symptoms, the cravings and headaches, irritability and tiredness.

Then, after three weeks of sticking to the new approach, something remarkable happened. Life became easier. She began to rarely feel tempted to overindulge. She actually enjoyed eating right. She lost weight again—and the pounds stayed off this time. Best of all, in discovering how she was wired, Nancy found something she had never felt and always sought before—freedom from the overeating-gaining-dieting-overeating-again cycle.

After three weeks of sticking to the new approach, something remarkable happened. Life became easier. She began to rarely feel tempted to overindulge.

"If I'd known sooner I was addicted to certain foods," Nancy said, "I could have been successful with weight loss instead of always losing the battle. I would have been better prepared to experience the withdrawals from sugar and bread. I would have been better equipped to handle the bodily and emotional discomfort. Just knowing I'm wired differently made the difference." Like Nancy, too many people who don't know they're food addicts blame themselves, and go through life feeling like failures.

Take the Test

Can knowing if your problem is willpower or wiring really unlock that kind of freedom for you? How can you tell if you're an actual food addict or have a dysfunctional relationship with sugar or high-calorie, high-fat foods? Some telltale signs of addiction are that you:

- exhibit tolerance. You need markedly increased amounts of food to achieve that "sugar high" or have markedly diminished effect with continued use of the same amount of food.
- experience characteristic withdrawal syndrome for food (cravings) or you substitute for food preoccupations with shopping, time spent on the Internet and social media, or sex to relieve or avoid withdrawal symptoms.
- often eat food in larger amounts or over a longer period than intended.

- persistently desire or unsuccessfully try to cut down or control eating too much.
- spend a great deal of time in activities necessary to obtain or use food or recover from its effects.
- give up social, occupational, or recreational activities because of food use.
- continue the food use with the knowledge it can worsen a persistent or recurrent physical or psychological problem.

Did any of those things sound familiar? Then take this quiz from the Yale Food Addiction Scale[1] and check any of the twenty-seven statements that apply to you:

1. When I start eating certain foods, I end up eating much more than planned.
2. I find myself continuing to consume certain foods even though I'm no longer hungry.
3. I eat to the point where I feel physically ill.
4. I worry about not eating certain types of food or cutting down on certain types of food.
5. I spend a lot of time feeling sluggish or fatigued from overeating.
6. I constantly eat certain foods throughout the day.
7. When certain foods aren't available, I'll go out of my way to obtain them. For example, I'll drive to the store to purchase certain foods even though I have other options available to me at home.
8. There have been times I consumed certain foods so often or in such large quantities I started to eat food instead of working, spending time with my family or friends, or engaging in other important activities or recreational activities I enjoy.
9. There have been times I consumed certain foods so often or in such large quantities I spent time dealing with negative feelings from overeating instead of working, spending time with my family or friends, or engaging in other important activities or recreational activities I enjoy.

10. There have been times I avoided professional or social situations where certain foods were available because I was afraid I would overeat.
11. There have been times I avoided professional or social situations because I was not able to consume certain foods there.
12. I have withdrawal symptoms such as agitation, anxiety, or other physical symptoms when I cut down or stopped eating certain foods. (Do not include withdrawal symptoms caused by cutting down on caffeinated beverages such as soda pop, coffee, tea, and energy drinks.)
13. I've consumed certain foods to prevent feelings of anxiety, agitation, or other physical symptoms that were developing.
14. I have urges to consume certain foods when I cut down or stop eating them.
15. My behavior with respect to food and eating causes significant distress.
16. I experience significant problems in my ability to function effectively (daily routine, job or school, social activities, family activities, and health difficulties) because of food and eating.

In the past twelve months . . .

17. My food consumption has caused significant psychological problems such as depression, anxiety, self-loathing, or guilt.
18. My food consumption has caused significant physical problems or made a physical problem worse.
19. I kept consuming the same types of food or the same amount of food even though I was having problems that were emotional, physical, or both.
20. Over time, I've needed to eat more and more to get the feeling I desire, such as reduced negative emotions or increased pleasure.
21. I've found eating the same amount of food does not reduce my negative emotions or increase pleasurable feelings the way it has in the past.

22. I want to cut down or stop eating certain kinds of food.
23. I've tried to cut down or stop eating certain kinds of food.
24. I've been successful at cutting down or not eating these kinds of food.
25. In the past year, I've tried to cut down or stop eating certain foods all together _____ times.
26. I've had problems with [circle all that apply]: Ice cream, Chocolate, Apples, Doughnuts, Broccoli, Cookies, Cake, Candy, White Rolls, Lettuce, Pasta, Strawberries, Rice, Crackers, Chips, Bread, Pretzels, French Fries, Carrots, Steak, Bananas, Bacon, Hamburgers, Cheese Fries, Burgers, Pizza, Soda Pop. None of these foods.
27. I've had problems with these other foods not previously listed: _____
_____
_____

You Can Rewire Success

The Yale researchers who created this test would say that even if you checked one of these twenty-seven statements, you're prone to food addiction. I would say something less drastic: you may have a food addiction or simply a dysfunctional relationship with food. So what are you to make of your survey results? How do you know if the way you're eating is some dysfunction or something more serious like an addiction?

We'll explore that, but let me first say this: Whether it's dysfunction or debilitation by addiction, how much do you want to hurt in your health, with your weight and your well-being? Are you okay with food causing you any amount of grief? Are you willing to keep on dealing with a problem whether it's small or severe?

If it's addiction you're facing, the consequences can be as serious as with alcohol and drugs because the cycle is ruining your life: your health with overweight, your finances with spending on diets that don't work and all the food to satisfy cravings, your peace of mind with the frustration, your very spirit with the shame.

If overeating and weight gain from how you eat is more a dysfunction but not debilitating, don't you still want to address it? It can be like a pebble in your shoe that doesn't cripple you but it irritates, causes some frustration and discomfort, and once removed allows you to go forward faster in life and with more ease. Doesn't that sound good?

Knowing where you are in the spectrum, and being honest and transparent in taking the quiz, means you've just taken your first

TRIGGER TALK

Two Brain Boosters

Athletes do two things to practice endurance that can help anyone dealing with food addiction or dysfunction issues when the withdrawal symptoms threaten to stop you:

- **Mine the Horizon Effect.** Focus on what's ahead. Look at not so much where you are or how much you have to do, as how far you've come and where you want to be. You'll be encouraged ("I've done twice as much as a week ago!") and newly determined ("I've made it this far, so I might as well keep going").
- **Refuse to turn goof-ups into give-ups.** You're just starting new things, you're just birthing new brain cells. How many times does a baby have to pronounce gobbledegook or single words before forming sentences? You don't stop just because of one hiccup. You keep on trying until you don't even have to think about the new thing you've grown brain cells to do. You'll get there, and each new success is truly remarkable!

important step toward recovery. Understanding how you're wired can help you recover from what has held you back and weighed you down all these years. You can finally work with your chemistry, not against it, to gain total freedom from food addiction.

It doesn't mean everyone else will understand. They won't. This is a fairly new revelation, and some professionals who treat eating disorders have yet to embrace what you'll need for recovery.

For instance, professionals treating eating disorders might advise Nancy to cut down on sugar and white flour—no need to completely eliminate them from her diet, just eat them in moderation. This is a more traditional eating disorders treatment model that says emotions, not foods themselves, are the primary problem. This model says food addictions will diminish as people learn better coping skills.

> **For the food addict, one bite of a trigger food can turn to many, and a cycle back into addiction.**

But this model doesn't address addiction issues at all. This model is what made Nancy, like so many of us with different brain wiring, feel like a failure, never fully recovering. This model says just one bite of a sugary treat is okay, when one bite of a sugary treat will never remain just one for Nancy, any more than one drink will stay at one drink for the alcoholic or one pill will satisfy the prescription drug addict. For the food addict, one bite of a trigger food can turn to many, and a cycle back into addiction.

Do you see what you've been up against?

No wonder you've been discouraged and deterred from living free from the insanity with food. But you're not crazy. You're not incapable of overcoming. You just need a different model for how to succeed. You need help with abstinence and addiction as much as, if not more than, willpower or determination. You need ways to refrain from eating sugar and other refined carbohydrates. You need help that starts in your head and heart, a new way of hardwired thinking of, feeling about, and behaving with food.

You Can Retrain Your Brain

You may have been taught you have all the brain cells you ever will have. Once they're gone, that's it. They don't grow back.

Well, guess what? Scientists now know that's simply wrong. Brain cells do grow back, just not exactly as they were in the beginning.[2] That's good news with startling, revolutionary implications for the rest of your life, especially if your brain is hardwired for addiction.

Here's how it works. Let's say you spend a lot of time in the business world. You're constantly computing profit and loss statements, looking at the bottom line of sales and expenses. Then, for whatever reason, you pursue a career in nursing. You use completely different skills, watching body functions and symptoms, extending compassion and care. The brain itself begins killing off the cells you once used for those business calculations. Two years later, a friend asks you to help start up a business and you find you're rusty in all that calculating and the quick sales reports you used to turn out in a day. It's not like the rote activity of riding a bicycle. You don't just jump back into the activity and turn out the same reports and statements without thinking. You need to retrain the brain cells for computing and calculating because for two years, your brain has been growing new cells, all devoted to caregiving.

Isn't this amazing? *The brain has been growing new cells.* Think of the implications of this new brain research for every one of us who struggle. If you can just do something different for a while, your brain will grow new cells trained for new behaviors. You can actually rewire your brain for better health.

I did, and so did Kim.

Of course, when Kim first called me she didn't know she would be working on her brain. She called about what she thought were body issues. She had heard an advertisement on the radio about food addiction treatment. The term was all new to her, but something about those words clicked. *Food. Addiction.* She thought of the times she needed a fix of not just one chocolate bar, but a whole package. The words, the idea, all made sense.

In our first meeting, Kim, forty-two, was about eighty pounds overweight and full of self-loathing—so much she'd suffered in silence for years. Finally talking openly about her shame brought immediate relief. So did learning that her struggle had a name—food addiction—and others suffered from it too. She was not a freak, nor alone. Others had overcome. This gave Kim the push she needed to change.

I urged her to attend a short intensive session where she learned about food dependency and the nuts and bolts of recovery. She started on a food plan where she weighed and measured what she ate, and removed all sugar and flour from her diet. She was surprised to find she could eat plenty of food on the plan and not feel like she was on a diet and deprived. Steering clear of the sweets and pastas she'd lived on for years took a period of adjustment, but as she stuck to the plan she noticed fewer cravings for sugar, flour, and excess food.

For the first time in years, Kim felt excitement and hope. *This might just work*, she remembers thinking. Food was falling into its proper place in her life. Instead of being consumed with thoughts of things to eat, she began to find energy to deal with all the underlying emotional, relational, and spiritual issues of her food addiction—issues she'd neglected for years. She joined both individual and group therapy and an additional 12-step group. She began to learn how to address her addiction at all levels, in her mind and body and soul. She began to rewire her brain. Rebuild her life. Restore her dreams. She was on the road to recovery and overcoming.

Now It's Your Turn

You can walk that road too. You can leave the sugar-loving rat race, get out of the dieting-and-demeaning hamster wheel. You just have to choose to address your head and heart and soul as much as your mouth and stomach. That's what facing food abuse and addiction is all about:

- You choose recovery over the raspberry cheesecake and ricotta-stuffed pasta.
- You want freedom more than French fries and Fat Burgers.
- You believe in life more than simply losing weight.
- You know your whole self matters more than any sugary snack.

So here's where we start looking at the things that trigger overeating: emotional responses, negative thinking, behavioral issues, spiritual floundering. You may find you've indulged in each of these things as much as any particular food. The bad news is they can affect your success as much as what you eat. The good news is you can turn things around. You can adjust your plans and mind-set, and refocus yourself, and you begin to transform your whole self by starting on the inside.

FOUR

The Science
of the Spirit

Deb, twenty-nine, called quickly after choosing to start on recovery. She was a week into committing to do whatever it took to stop overeating and she couldn't wait another day. She had been fighting with food issues more years of her life than she could remember, and she yearned to be free from it all. The battle began when she was ten and her father, with a hand on her head, introduced her to new neighbors as, "This is Deb, our chubby one."

"*Our chubby one!*" Deb said in our first meeting. "Dad may as well have knighted me Deb the Chubby One because that is exactly the code I lived by every day after."

As she reached to food for comfort, that code brought on even more pounds, not peace. Finally, ready to stop the binges, stop the focus again and again on her body (how to slim it with doomed diets, how to hide it with outlandish fashion), Deb called ahead of our scheduled appointment. Anything she could start doing, even thinking on, to change her life?

"I'm already looking into food plans," she said, "and you'll help me take on all the issues that drive me to overeat and binge, right?"

"Right," I answered, "and we'll work on ways to strengthen your spirit too."

"My . . . spirit?" It was like Deb had never heard the word. There was a long silence before she said, "Come again?"

"We'll look at ways God can help you." More silence. *Odd,* I thought. Deb was a Christian. We knew mutual friends at her church. Matters of faith weren't unknown to her. Still, I explained, "There are things you can do to strengthen your spirit that will give you the freedom you seek." More silence. "You know," I filled in, "how prayer, meditation on God's Word, and faith in His promises will help you overcome and find peace with what you eat."

The silence was even more palpable this time. Longer. Long enough that I thought the call had dropped or maybe I should cue the crickets. Then I heard a breath, a slight shuffling. "Deb? Are you there? Are you okay?"

"I thought you said, 'we'll look at spiritual things,'" she answered slowly, deliberately, as if trying on the words and not finding them a fit. There was another long pause.

"That's right."

Silence.

"Is something wrong?"

"Well," Deb said, as if the reins had been pulled on her gallop toward recovery, "I just didn't think this was going to be so complicated. I understand recovery isn't just about a diet. I get that the brain is involved, there are triggers, and there are emotions to deal with, but, really, what do prayer and meditation have to do with my eating problem? What does faith have to do with food issues anyway?"

What does faith have to do with food, with issues, with addiction, with freedom?

In a word: everything.

Faith Helps You Heal

The evidence is substantial for what people have believed for centuries: faith helps you heal.[1] There's power in prayer. Meditation on God's Word brings peace. Gathering with fellow believers delivers belonging and supplies support.

There's a whole biology of belief on the way faith affects your physical, emotional, and mental self.[2] The bottom line is simple: God is great. He's good. He's good for you in every way. Relationship with Him not only saves your soul; how you practice your faith in God helps your body, your mind, and your emotions too.

For instance, look at just a few of the benefits recently found in the groundbreaking research at the University of Pennsylvania's Center for Spirituality and the Mind:[3]

- **Spiritual practice reduces stress.**
- **Contemplation of a loving God can curtail anxiety** and depression.
- **Time spent talking to, thinking upon, and worshipping God increases feelings** of security, compassion, and love.
- **Prayer enlivens and activates your senses** by involving your sensory organs for taste, sight, smell, sound—so you engage more fully in what is going on around you, as well as inside you, your thoughts, and feelings.
- **Prayer deepens your capacity for gratitude,** which, like humor, can boost your immune system and resiliency.
- **Meditation has lasting effects on the functioning of the brain,** including changing values and perception of reality.
- **People who attend church services live longer** than those who don't.
- **Belief in a loving God helps you handle a diagnosis of illness and fare better afterward** than no belief or a belief that God is punitive.

The benefits go on and seem almost too good to be true, but the proof is too convincing to think otherwise. Exercising your faith really is just what the Good Doctor ordered for peace, fitness, total health, and a vibrant, full life. And the best part of it? You can be part of the living proof. You can grab on to faith's benefits and see your whole life change for good because faith is the key to freedom from food addiction, mad cycles of eating, and all the aftereffects like weight gain, debilitating guilt and shame, and low self-worth. Practices of faith can bring you

- **healing** for an overweight body and overburdened mind;
- **power to overcome** any challenge;
- **peace** as you face your past; and
- **a community of support** to help when you're sick, tired, or discouraged and to celebrate good moments and great days with you.

Faith will enable the mental clarity you need to make good decisions in all situations and get you through tough times. Faith also gives you what you won't get from your body or your mind—a super strength and sustenance of the soul that is the true ingredient to overcoming.

Faith is the key to freedom from food addiction.

While the evidence of this is fascinating, step back a minute and think about what you already know beyond the science of the soul. We've all read accounts of people on the brink of physical and mental collapse, who then persevere and get through an ordeal or challenge by sheer faith and an indomitable spirit. You probably know more examples than you realize of those who overcame great obstacles by exercising faith, in spite of physical, emotional, and mental limitations.

Remember Corrie ten Boom, the middle-aged, unmarried clockmaker who joined the Dutch Resistance during World War II? Corrie hid in her home, many of those hunted by the Nazis, and helped save the lives of hundreds of Jews and people of the Resistance before being interned with them. At age forty-eight, she endured eleven months at Ravensbruck Concentration Camp, and lost most of her family, before being released by clerical error (one week, by the way, before all women her age were killed). Then, despite the lasting physical and emotional effects of her starvation and torture, she devoted the rest of her ninety-one years to helping other survivors. She set up rehabilitation centers, sheltered the jobless Dutch who had collaborated with the Germans during the occupation, and traveled the world as a public speaker and author.

At a speaking engagement in Munich, she came face-to-face

with one of her tormenters from the camps . . . and forgave him. She *forgave* the man who helped persecute her and kill her eighty-four-year-old father and sister Betsie, who saw to it she and those with her suffered in the camps. People were stunned. Corrie was too. How could she do such a thing? Where does one summon that kind of spirit to defy physical limitation (Corrie often joked she was a little dumpling, no athlete)? How does one overcome the anger, bitterness, and agony of grief to do so?

It wasn't her body that enabled her to travel all those miles, all those years, with her message of hope. It wasn't her mind and heart, forever grieved by loss, that allowed her to pardon her persecutor. It was her faith. It was God. "I stood there . . . and could not forgive," she wrote. "I had to do it." She prayed silently and "healing warmth seemed to flood my whole being"—not her own love, but "the power of the Holy Spirit."[4] Doing the impossible freed her from imprisoning emotions, and it was her spirit, her faith in God, that made possible the impossible.

That same spirit, so intimately connected to God, enabled Corrie to keep singing His praises the last five years of her life when a series of strokes left her bedridden and mute. Though she couldn't speak or write, she continued to signal her trust in and love for God with eye motions, in response to Bible readings, prayers, and gestures from her caretaker and friends.[5] Corrie's body was stilled, imprisoned by effects of those strokes, but her spirit, by faith, was free and vibrant as ever.

That kind of faith is what helps overcome torment and whatever has isolated and imprisoned anyone in the mad cycle with food addiction and issues. Where the body says, *This is too exhausting, too taxing*, the spirit can will another step. Where the mind says, *I can't go on, I can't deal with this*, the spirit enables going on anyway, pushing through regardless.

Faith, we see in Hebrews, is the thing that got a cloud of witnesses (Hebrews 12:1) through all kinds of dark valleys and shadows of death. Faith is what, when the body fails and mind falters, gets you over a hump, up a hill, and ahead of what is better left behind.

TRIGGER TALK
How to Trigger a Taste for God

So you see now how faith practices help you be more fit in mind, body, and spirit. Here are the best ways I've seen (and experienced in my own life) to trigger those practices so they become habits—and the habits become your lifestyle.

- **Start the day with God.** As soon as you wake, ask God to go with you hour by hour, to direct your thinking away from self-pity or anything self-serving and toward what's right and good. Ask Him to guide your choices.

- **Meditate upon Him.** Sit somewhere quiet to let go of racing thoughts and focus. Still yourself to release other desires. Close your eyes to shut out distraction and help you look within. Think upon a word, or certain words, for instance, a phrase from the Lord's prayer (Matthew 6:9–13: "Our Father who is in heaven, hallowed be Your name") or the names of God (*Counselor. Redeemer. Provider.*). Repeat these words or phrases, in your mind or aloud, for several minutes. Say them slowly and deliberately, breathing deeply and staying focused, letting go of self-analysis and instead focusing on the words of God.

- **Deepen your relationship with God**. Make dates to spend time with Him daily. Start by getting to know who He is, His character. Read devotionals and books of daily meditation on Him that will help you fall and stay in love with Him and worship Him. Some of the books that helped me most are the daily readers in 12-step programs; and classics like *My Utmost for His Highest* by Oswald Chambers, *Jesus Calling* by Sarah Young, *Streams in the Desert* by L. B. E. Cowman (and the updated edition edited by James Reimann), and *The Battlefield of the Mind Devotional* and *The Confident Woman Devotional* by Joyce Meyer. The book that helped me most, giving me spiritual food for daily living, is *Experiencing the Depths of Jesus Christ* by a seventeenth-century woman, Jeanne-Marie Bouvier de la Motte-Guyon, commonly known as Madame Guyon—this slim but meaty book helped me fill up on God rather than food. Her book *A Short and Easy Method of Prayer*, available in many forms, even free online, also helps you practice in very practical ways how to have a conversation with God anywhere, anytime, and be in His presence—and it leads to another way of plugging in to the power of the spiritual solution. The Life Recovery Bible with commentary from David Stoop, PhD, and Stephen Arterburn, MEd, is helpful too, including additional model perspectives in devotionals, serenity prayers, and encouraging reflections from and profiles of people in recovery.

- **Pray.** Just as one bite of a chip can lead to eating the whole bag, one prayer triggers many. Keep a conversation going with God through the day. Be deliberate. Pray at appointed times: before meals, upon leaving work, as you go to bed. Use the structure of the Lord's Prayer as a guide: Address God and acknowledge His goodness, His holiness. Ask for His will for this day. Tell Him what you need. Thank Him for help you believe He will deliver. Ask for forgiveness of things done and left undone. Ask Him to help you forgive others, and for guidance and wisdom to get through the next twenty-four hours. Thank Him for His goodness.

- **Feed on the Bible.** Read Scripture like you eat a meal, not in snippets or as a snack, but as a full course, a story, a letter from God to you. It means making time in your day, as you would for a meal, to read a section of the Bible, not just a verse. Choose one chapter or several. Ask: Who is this about, for, from? What happens or is said? What does this mean for me? How can I use this in my life today, this week? A wonderful tool on getting the most from your Bible reading is Kay Arthur's short book *How to Read the Bible* (Harvest House), which offers five helpful practices in fewer than 180 pages.

The fascinating thing is faith can actually help your body survive what it says it can't. Faith can help your mind process and handle what it says you shouldn't.

HOW BELIEF AFFECTS BIOLOGY

So exactly how does it work? Can one's faith and the practice of it really create physical, mental, and emotional change? Can belief enable you to overcome eating issues, get healthier in every way, do anyway what your body and mind may signal they cannot?

Yes! By God's design there is a science to the soul, and belief does affect biology.

For fifteen years, neuroscientist Andrew Newberg, M.D., and therapist Mark Waldman looked into this and helped pioneer a whole new field called "neurotheology."[6] They studied brain scans, interviewed thousands of people in surveys, and analyzed how people depicted God in drawings, plus what happened in those people's brains as they engaged in how God showed up to them on a page in their art and in their everyday lives.

Their discoveries, detailed in their book *How God Changes Your Brain*, are electric, literally visible. Newberg and Waldman show how pathways in the brain "light up" when people pray, worship, or even talk and think about God. The more you use a part of the brain encountering religion, they explain, the more blood flow it gets and the brighter red in color those parts appear on brain scans. When you engage, exercise, and feed your spirit, visible effects show in your head and through your body.

Believing Builds up Brain Pathways
For starters, when you even think of God, certain pathways in your brain actually grow, enlarge, strengthen, open, and activate your thought processes and bodily behavior. That's what the researchers mean, in addition to what shows on the brain scans, by those pathways "lighting up." These pathways respond to religious practice just

like body movement makes the heart pump faster. There's a direct connection between the body and thought processes and the brain, an unmistakable influence. Your body and mind are definitely affected by the matters of your spirit, and the very act of believing, in and of itself, changes brain structure.

One of those effects or changes brought about by belief shows up as a kind of power—power that heals and helps you in every way.

In a way, it's sort of like a placebo effect. You know about placebos. People fighting disease or illness can be given a placebo, a pill or treatment with zero therapeutic property and still get better, heal, or experience less pain simply because they believed in the medicine. Yet the medicine itself offered no power. The belief in it did.

The act of believing in a loving God seems to activate the same kind of power. People who carry out spiritual practices based on their beliefs handle disease and illness better than those who don't.[7] That's not to say believers in a good God don't get sick, die, or suffer. It is saying that the science shows how the very act of believing God is good, and that His promises will help you in this life and beyond it, ushers in more ability to fare better physically and mentally. Sometimes believers did well by experiencing peace of mind and spirit amid the physical punishment of illness and disease, sometimes by possessing serenity in spite of suffering, and, yes, sometimes with improved health and healing.[8]

Isn't that encouraging?

If people who believe in a fake treatment get positive results by the act of believing alone, imagine how much more you can expect to receive when you focus your belief on the Almighty God who, regardless of whether you believe in Him or not, holds the power to give you every breath you take.

Prayer Powers Your Brain Up and Down

Practicing such belief gives you more of this benefit and power as actual brain structure is changed. When you pray, for instance, the frontal lobes of your brain take the lead to deliver literal brain power.

Those frontal lobes govern your ability to focus and concentrate, so praying activates the same brain passages that help you find clarity and be more mindful, deliberate, engaged, and thoughtful. Praying powers up the brain to think clearly and sort through things.

Prayer also calms your brain in the very best way. Deep, intense prayer engages the parietal lobe, the part of the brain that gives you orientation to space and time. When you pray fervently and feverishly the parietal lobes essentially power down, creating a euphoric, ethereal state. This enables you to feel loosed from a situation, able to rise above the circumstances. Your body's relaxed, your mind is opened and unencumbered, and you're freed from what might otherwise paralyze you emotionally.

Meditation Fosters Memory, Decision Making, Calm, and Compassion

The brain is activated even more by meditation. If the very word *meditation* makes you think of people in yoga pants sitting in a circle and chanting "om," that's only one picture.

For meditation, one person in the study may have used Eastern religion techniques like what you envisioned, and terms like "silence the mind" and "breathe deeply." But others used what we typically do as Christians in our devotional times—what Jesus, the prophets, disciples, and ancients used to think on to connect with God. With this type of meditation you:

- **separate yourself from distraction** by going to a quiet place. Jesus often withdrew to the lonely places and wilderness for time with God.
- **still your body and thoughts.** David, the shepherd-king who wrote a whole book of psalms and meditations, said in Psalm 37:7 how good it is to find God in stillness.
- **think intently on God**, dwell on Him, connect with Him (Eastern religions might suggest more vaguely to think on "things higher"). The prophets, Jesus, disciples, and many

others throughout the Old and New Testament constantly and consistently talked to God through prayer, whether it was silent or spoken or written or sung in praises and in music. They strove to keep Him ever present in their hearts.

• **ponder deeply, relish the experience of connecting with the Maker of the universe.** Brother Lawrence, a fifteenth-century monk in Paris, talked about experiencing God in simple, almost rote tasks of service performed as prayers and done in love—in everyday tasks such as washing pots and pans in the kitchen or repairing sandals and shining shoes.[9]

Thirty minutes of meditation practices a day, for as little as eight weeks, created actual changes in brain structure. One study showed the frontal lobes of people's brains bulked up.[10] Another showed the cerebral cortex, the outermost layer of neural tissue, not only thickened, but folded more, a process called gyrification.[11] Both changes increased brain power. The more the frontal lobes of the brain bulked up and the more gyrification that occurred, the better the brain became at processing information, making decisions, and forming memories.

Other things happened in meditation too. A unique central neural circuit in the brain was switched on, enabling social awareness, empathy, and compassion, while also subduing destructive feelings and emotions.

HOW THE BIOLOGY OF BELIEF HELPS YOU

This couldn't be better news for people fighting food issues. Once you decide to finally confront a food addiction and face the triggers, you must make all kinds of new decisions. You'll need to think clearly and be able to process a lot of new information for a new life. There will come a time when all the guilt and shame you've felt by hiding those binges, all the torment of carrying that weight, all the confusion and pain of dealing with the emotional issues that drove you to overeat to begin with, will seem too much to bear. You'll long for peace. You'll need to learn all new things about self-care, compassion, and being kind to yourself.

All this can overwhelm you . . . unless you know you have God on your side, until you realize tuning in to Him will help you in every way. By His design, He gave you things you can do to power up the brain, engage your best emotions, soothe your soul, and rely on Him where you can't rely on anything or anyone else.

Deb discovered this with her first phone call, taking those first steps on the road to recovery. She thought she needed to go right to work on the things regarding her body and maybe her mind, her emotions. But instead we talked about things of the spirit.

"The body can fail and your brain can falter," Deb said, as if trying on an idea that finally fit. "But your spirit can overcome. That is so encouraging, because I called you knowing my physical and emotional limitations were huge. I guess I was hoping you could give me some sort of diet pill or prescription or something to make everything better. Frankly, I've tried so hard for so long to change on my own, and I keep going back to the fast food and the desserts. I keep on with binges. My body has failed and my brain has faltered. I can't trust my emotions. I can't do this alone."

None of us can.

> **We don't need to have our lives in order to go to God. We need God to help us get our lives in order.**

We are not meant to face this life, and all its challenges, alone. We are meant to face every moment with God by our side. We are meant to call on Him for help and use all the tools He gives us, designed for us. We are meant to know His promise, His love, and the unique master plan He has for each of us. A plan that cares about food and relationships and health, but is bigger than all those things put together. "Plans to prosper you and not to harm you," He says (Jeremiah 29:11 NIV), "plans to give you hope and a future."

Deb sighed. "I know that about God," she said. "I know He's good, and He loves me. It's why I'm so ashamed. I've messed up so much."

We all have. We all do. But we don't need to have our lives in order to go to God. We need God to help us get our lives in order.

This is the challenge, especially for those of us battling addictions, and those of us who have latched on to this idea through untrue religion or wrong thinking, that we have to comprehend. We've somehow believed we have to clean up our acts before God will love us. Nothing could be more opposite of the truth. If we could get clean, get fixed, find healing, stop the madness, be complete, and attain perfection without God, we would have already. But no one has, and no one will.

God loves us anyway, in spite of, and because of, just who we are. It's why He made sure, even though we may make bad choices, we can overcome them by His design. He's made us able to be strengthened by our belief in His power, and to experience the power of that belief. He has given us a way to become stronger and more whole by practicing our belief in His unconditional love and grace. He knows we'll succumb to a cupcake now and then, and maybe not just one but a dozen or twenty at a time. He knows we'll struggle with self-worth and guilt and shame. He doesn't expect us to get our act together before coming to Him for help. He just wants us to pray, meditate upon His Word, make time each day to simply be with Him and enjoy Him, and tell Him our troubles. In doing these things, in practicing our belief, there are benefits, both biological and spiritual.

With all the things you'll learn about in this book regarding how to live that plan, keep coming back to this spiritual solution!

PART TWO

The Heart and Soul of Your Triggers

Search me, O God, and know my heart; try me and know my anxious thoughts . . . and lead me in the everlasting way.

—PSALM 139:23–24

FIVE

Looking for Love in All the Wrong Places

I find so powerful the scene in the movie *What Women Want* where Nick Marshall (played by Mel Gibson) struggles with his feelings for Darcy McGuire (played by Helen Hunt). Nick begins to like and then care deeply for Darcy. He's falling in love and doesn't even know it. After years of seeing women as simply for his pleasure, these new feelings of devotion and commitment to a woman are strange. They scare Nick when he begins to think of giving more consideration to Darcy than himself. He has only known how to use, then lose track of woman after woman who gave him what he wanted for the moment: a kiss, an idea, some inspiration, some flattery, a fling.

Confused, Nick wanders into the kitchen. He's searching for . . . he doesn't know what. He's flailing about, opens the refrigerator, looks around, then, suddenly aware, mutters to himself, "She's not in there."

Wow. What a moment of recognition. How many times do we look in the fridge for what we thought we want? How often, instead of dealing with our issues and relationships, do we turn to food? How regularly do we reach for dessert after dessert or carton after container of some trigger food to satisfy us, even for just the moment?

Plenty, admits Sara, thirty-six, and single.

Even a few years into recovery, Sara found herself one evening like Nick, with a hand on the opened refrigerator door. Remembering how she stared down the condiments, yogurt, and a bag of salad, she says, "Thank goodness the cheesecake I once kept stocked all the time wasn't there. I had been keeping to a healthy food plan, so I'd learned long ago to clean out all the things I would otherwise devour in such a moment."

But while she had cleaned out the kitchen of trigger foods, she was only just beginning to learn about needing to clean out her inner self and deal with the emotional issues that drew her to use food for comfort in the first place. It's why, when the pangs of loneliness seized her, instinctively, Sara still ran to the refrigerator. Only this time, suddenly, as if the switch on the radio had been flipped by the open door, she heard the refrain of an old country song. "Lookin' for love in all the wrong places . . . Hopin' to find a friend and a lover. . . ."

I'm not hungry for food. I'm hungry for love.

What I really want isn't in here, Sara realized, and, like Nick, she knew: *I'm not hungry for food. I'm hungry for love.*

FOOD CAN NEVER FILL YOUR SOUL

What you need and want most is not in the refrigerator or the cupboard, from a grocery shelf, or on a menu. What you need and want most are often the things that haven't come to you easily or at all: love, belonging, security, success, fulfilling relationships, meaning.

Maybe you're like Sara or Nick and alone, wanting love but not yet finding it. Or maybe you're married but the relationship's growing distant, loveless, lifeless. Maybe your family is filled more with friction and disconnection than belonging and support. Maybe you want to make a difference in this world, but aren't seeing how what you do matters in your work. Maybe you're out of work and feeling rejected or like a failure. Maybe you want a friend and don't have one or know how to be one or make one.

No matter how you slice it, the things you want most in life can elude you completely or seem too hard to get. Food, on the other hand, can be everywhere and easy to find most of the time. Somewhere in the search for what you've longed for most in life, you've turned to food to fill the empty places.

Think about it. Your turn may have started innocently enough. Maybe you had a terrible day and someone took you for ice cream as

TRIGGER TALK

Map Your Success

What can help you walk away from the fridge when you find yourself in Nick's shoes, ready to dig in to something to eat you don't need? This is such a critical junction and maybe you've never thought it through before, but it's going to help you now.

You're at a crossroads. Play out this idea in your mind. There are two different path choices here, and one makes all your plans go south, while the other builds you up, leads you forward, and helps you get to your goals.

Make a visual reminder of this. Print a picture from online, tear one from a magazine, or simply draw one of a crossroads. On the way going south, the one where you eat for no good reason, write down where this road leads: to binges, weight gain, guilt, shame. Add how this journey feels: entangled, guilt-ridden, shameful, bumpy, up and down, full of potholes and drop-offs.

Now write down where the upward road leads: no overeating, boosted confidence in sticking to your plans, a retraining of the brain, no more guilt and shame. How does traveling this road feel? Maybe not easy but smoother, gentler, less encumbered with things that stop you from where you want to go, open, free.

It's a picture to keep handy, showing you exactly which way to go when you're feeling a bit lost. Now you know what to do. That's right: walk away from the fridge.

a way of cheering or soothing you. There's a reason for the term *comfort food*. The ice cream tasted good and the kindness involving it did indeed comfort, relieve, and cheer you. The sweet treat replaced the pain of whatever you were missing with pleasure, for the moment anyway. Then because it worked once, the next time you had a bad day or terrible experience you turned to ice cream again, and again, each time wanting the same relief, which you got . . . until the next time you had a bad day or situation.

In the meantime, going for ice cream became habitual, and the ice cream itself became a friend to help you cope.

Ice cream, however, like any go-to food, is a false friend. Ice cream melts. It leaves you. It's fickle, fair-weathered, and untrue. By its very nature, it's a temporal thing. It cannot sustain you for long, and once burned needs replenishing, and if not burned turns into fat, which doesn't sustain at all but debilitates one spoonful at a time. Food doesn't fix what's wrong in your spirit, and the only way it is a fix at all is like any substance used by an addict. The substance can't solve anything. Rather it extends the misery, sugarcoats reality, and offers temporary escape from what is better confronted. So while you think your go-to food gives you something good, instead it leaves you with all the same bad feelings as before you ate, plus so much more: guilt, shame, a strengthened trigger for more of what you thought was satisfying and really wasn't, really can't be.

You know the cycle.

So does everyone else. Turning to food in a crisis is not just our own experience, but also our culture's, which encourages the illusion sweets can soothe the soul. Feeding frustration, sadness, hurt, and disappointment with food, in fact, has become a national joke. How many times have you heard someone laughingly say, "When the going gets tough, the tough get chocolate"? How many T-shirts and bumper stickers have you seen emblazoned: "Forget love. I want to fall in chocolate"? How many Boynton greeting cards have you sent or received with the cute hippo pleading, "Things are getting worse. Send chocolate"?[1]

British comedienne Dawn French actually works to develop such scenarios for her characters. "I never do any television without chocolate," she says. "It's my motto and I live by it. Quite often I write the scripts and I make sure there are chocolate scenes."[2] Her character as the single woman vicar, in the BBC series *Vicar of Dibley*, wears a coat lined with chocolate bars, keeps cupboards stuffed with candy, and hoards ice cream. She gets lots of laughs when, troubled or stressed, she whips open her coat of chocolates, reveals a secret compartment in her Bible for candy bars, or lunges for the freezer filled with Ben & Jerry's.

So the studio audience laughs at the bingeing, but the truth behind it is far from funny. It's tragic, as Edmund Pevensie discovers in C. S. Lewis's beloved book *The Lion, the Witch, and the Wardrobe*.[3] Edmund, frustrated and angry because his older brother and sisters don't take him seriously, stomps off into a wintery wilderness into which they've stumbled. He plunges deeper and deeper into the strange forest, uncharted territory, fuming his siblings don't respect him. Finally, vulnerable and alone, he meets the White Witch, who offers him a hot drink and his favorite candy, Turkish Delight. Edmund is surprised by what seems a kindness, good fortune, when the candy is piled into his hands in an ornate box tied with silky green ribbon. He opens the box and seizes one of the gem-like delights. He bites into it hungrily, then another and another. The sweets bewitch him. One taste leads to the want for more, and soon Edmund finds himself running to the White Witch's ice castle to sell his soul, betraying the very ones he loves for . . . candy.

Too late, Edmund discovers that trying once to soothe his rumpled feelings with sugar has become a terrible pattern and led to the destruction of all he holds dear: his own self, family, and very world. Even Turkish Delight, the confection of the rich and the royals, cannot fill him with respect or take away his angst, just as chocolate cannot replace love, or pudding cannot deliver purpose and progress, or brownies take the place of a boyfriend or fix marriage woes.

Emotional hunger is not sated by ice cream and cookies or choc-olate and peanut butter. To think we can feed the spirit and our emo-tions with food is like walking straight into the White Witch's ice dungeon; the trap leads only to a prison where we ache more severely than when set off in search of something satisfying. Only God can fill us with the meaning, purpose, love, and belonging we seek. Fill-ing up on Him first is where satisfaction begins and ends.

"I am the bread of life," Jesus promises (John 6:35 NIV). "Who-ever comes to me will never go hungry, and whoever believes in me will never be thirsty." He will fill us in every way. He knows we physi-cally need food and water for suste-nance, evidenced by His miracle in John 6 of feeding the hungry with fishes and loaves. But only He can fill what your heart, mind, and soul truly crave. It's why when He prom-ises the bread of life, He's talking about so much more than hot rolls or barley loaves and baguettes, and it's why He wants you to know the difference between an empty stomach and an empty heart. Tend to your heart (your feelings) and your mind (your choices), and you won't confuse filling your belly with food as a way of satiating what you're really craving when you go to the fridge because you're lonely or feeling abandoned or looking for love.

> **Tend to your heart (your feelings) and your mind (your choices), and you won't confuse filling your belly with food as a way of satiating what you're really craving.**

SEPARATING THE HUNGERS OF MOOD AND FOOD

When you've struggled with food addiction, knowing what you're really hungry for, recognizing the difference between physical and emotional hunger, is a huge challenge. For so long you've been trig-gered not just by food, but by feelings. Your emotions have driven you to take the first bite of a trigger food for comfort, and then because you're hardwired for addiction you've stayed that course to eat and eat and eat to fill emptiness and satiate pain.

Like Edmund, you've been bewitched. You've chased after what you thought would bring relief and when one taste triggered more, you didn't keep eating because you were hungry. You kept eating because you were empty. There's a difference, but one you smothered so long ago you may not recognize it anymore.

When Sara looked back on the moment she stood at the refrigerator door and realized what she wanted was love and not lemon cheesecake, she began to find the difference. She began to separate a food trigger from an emotional one. "Understanding that loneliness set me off emotionally suddenly became as important to me as the food plan," she said. "Certain emotions are what drove me to overeat to begin with, so recognizing it was like being handed a remote control for my life. I realized I really could change the channel, stop the reruns of turning to food or anything else instead of confronting what was going on inside me. The change I needed was to not only eat well, but live well by dealing with my heart."

The good news? You can relearn the difference between physical and emotional hunger.

To start, think on how the pangs of physical hunger and emotional hurt can feel so much the same: the pounding in your head, ache in your heart, yawning hollowness in the pit of your stomach, tightness in your throat, burning and gnawing inside your chest. Isn't it strangely similar, the sensation of needing food for your stomach and sustenance for your spirit—those times you feel lonely, rejected, grieved, bitter, abandoned, or hurt? Both hungers can leave you feeling the same: faint, weary, and weak.

But physical and emotional hunger differ too in several ways:

- **Emotional hunger doesn't notice signs of fullness but physical hunger can be satiated** and you can stop eating when you're full. With the emotional, even when your stomach is full, you keep eating until you're numb to what triggered the impulse to eat.

- **Emotional eating doesn't satisfy and leaves you feeling ashamed and guilty,** while there's no remorse when you satisfy physical hunger and no guilt in eating.
- **Emotional hunger must be fed by what you crave but physical hunger can be satiated by most any food,** from spinach to sauerkraut, even foods you don't especially enjoy by taste or texture. With emotional eating you want your trigger foods, whether they're sweet like ice cream and doughnuts or high-fat and savory like pizza and potato chips.
- **Emotional hunger arrests you suddenly but physical hunger grows gradually.** With emotional hunger, there's an intense, urgent impulse to eat, and you confuse an emotional need for a physical one. The need isn't really for food but you can't seem to get food off your mind, and once you start eating you can't seem to stop. Physical hunger begins with subtle cues like a growling stomach and can grow to a yawning feeling in your stomach and eventually a headache and light-headedness. For the most part, however, you can control these signals, deciding when to eat and when to stop.

When you begin to recognize them, Sara admitted, the differences seem so obvious. "You see patterns of not just the foods that have triggered you to overeat, but the circumstances."

You begin to see, as Nick did, that what may pull you to the refrigerator is not just the cupcake but a kiss, not only a batch of fudge but a fling. Your soul hungers for something more satisfying beyond what's immediately there for the taking, for the moment. Because you want more from life, you start paying attention to not only what you're eating, but what's eating you.[4]

SIX

What Is Eating You?

I f Nick Marshall or Sara or Edmund Pevensie could have been handed a scrapbook showing the turning points of their lives, they might begin to discover their emotional triggers. Nick would see a snapshot of commitment with Darcy and not just a kiss with any other woman. Sara would find a picture of companionship with someone she loved who loved her back. Edmund would have an illustration of his brother and sisters going along with him in regard and respect.

Wouldn't you like to know so clearly, see so easily the moods or circumstances and issues that have troubled you over time and made you reach again and again for food?

While the process of discovering your emotional triggers won't be so easy, it can be clear and it will be freeing. Like Sara described, it will be like being given a remote control for your life, flipping from the reruns of madness with food and episodes of overeating, binge-ing, and feeling under food's control, to living unscripted and without fear and shame. You can hold a scrapbook of sorts that reveals your emotional triggers.

LOOK AT YOUR LIFE ON PAPER

One of the best methods for this kind of self-discovery that I've found is to write out the turning points in your life. You don't have to be a writer to do this. You simply need to be willing to put on paper the significant events you remember about the first time you

- **binged;**
- **grieved over a great loss;**
- **heard someone say something cutting** about your appearance or eating habits, patterns, or acts; or
- **felt ashamed of eating** or hid your eating.

By chronicling such things on paper, you allow yourself a closer look at them. You enable yourself to identify what prompted your turn to food for comfort or control. You begin to see the patterns of behavior, including both triggers and the effects of succumbing to them. This sets you on a healing journey of finally dealing with whatever you've used food to ignore, bury, or hide in secrecy and shame. It gives you an undeniable and stark look at—and, yes, it can be hard—unresolved grief, loss, bitterness, abandonment, rejection, trauma, and other issues.

Without such a look, you can go on like my client Tom. At age fifty, Tom was at least one hundred pounds overweight. He had trouble getting in and out of the chair in my office, but while he admitted he had a weight problem, he denied being a food addict or overeating. "I'm happily married with loving children," he said. "I just needed help losing weight."

We talked about what he ate and when, and he told me about reasonable breakfasts, lunches, and dinners.

"What else?" I prodded. A person doesn't keep on that kind of weight with such regular portions of food and activity.

"Nothing more," Tom insisted.

So we agreed for him to keep a food journal. At the end of a week, not only could I see, but Tom saw as well, he was indeed eating reasonable breakfasts, lunches, and dinners—and in-between also unbelievable amounts of snacks and desserts, one handful, spoonful, sack, and carton at a time. In fact, Tom couldn't deny he was eating more than three meals a day. He was eating all through the day, one long continuous smorgasbord. The notes on paper from just one week of his life spoke volumes.

He finally agreed he might have a food addiction.

"Let's look closer," I suggested. "Let's consider all the emotions or issues from the past that have contributed to this."

Tom couldn't believe emotions or past events were the problem. "It's what's going on with me now that I need help with," he said. "I don't know why I can't lose weight." He wanted help dieting. He asked for help in strengthening his willpower. He was trapped in all the typical misunderstandings about food issues.

"Let's try the process of looking at past events and emotions," I insisted. "Just as a food journal has a story to tell, so does looking at your life on paper. Snapshots of the significant events and turning points in your life will tell how you got here." I didn't say it because Tom wasn't ready to hear it yet, but I knew neither willpower nor diet issues were at the crux of his story.

With reluctance, Tom agreed. By the second question, all kinds of answers about why he overate began to surface.

What is your first memory of overeating?

Immediately Tom recalled when he was twelve taking a box of snack crackers, sack of potato chips, and a cherry pie to his bedroom, shutting the door, and eating every bit in one sitting.

What was going on with your family at that time?

Tom's parents had just divorced. He was living with his mom, who began to work outside their home, so he was on his own a lot for the first time in his life. He rarely saw his dad anymore, though it was okay, he said, because his father had begun to mock him for what he now knows was attention deficit disorder, but then was just thought of by a schoolteacher as bad behavior. The kids at school were teasing him about being on the move all the time. "Tom the Ping-Pong, they called me," he wrote.

Then beneath all this, he added, "I grew up feeling helpless and horrible and wanting to die."

Wow. This was like seeing a big message written in orange smoke across the sky. I expected him to see the message clearly too: how the cycle of overeating began, where food became the solace he sought instead of family, how he ate for pleasure to cover his inner pain.

But Tom wasn't persuaded. "What does then have to do with now?" he pressed. He didn't want to die now. He had a loving family, a wife and two daughters. He just needed to lose weight. He just needed to stop overeating. *Then*, of course, has everything to do with *now*. Every time Tom needed encouragement or felt bad about himself, was insecure or felt threatened in any way by an authority figure like his mocking and distant father, he returned to all those childhood feelings and his solution of food for comfort. As Tom plotted more events on a timeline about when he overate and what was going on before and after those times, the cycle and circumstances he'd denied for years became very apparent.

Mapping the events of his life on paper became the tool that unlocked recovery for Tom. It can help you too, but be warned: this can be hard work. You may not want to do it, just as Tom was reluctant to. You're going to question and doubt if this is where you'll find the answers for how and why you eat as you do or keep on weight and wrestle with wellness. So I say to you what I said to Tom: take a look, be open and willing to explore these things, and be patient with the process. Each of these steps will get you closer to freedom.

Mark the Signposts

Here are some of the most effective ways of identifying the turning points in your life:

- **Make a traditional timeline.** Draw out one long horizontal line on paper, and make short vertical dots on it, plotting each turning point in your life from birth to the present and all the significant events in between: First relationships, school memories, trials or tragic events, moves and transitions.
- **Create a collapsible timeline** by writing on sheets of paper those specific memories of firsts and significant events, one page at a time for each thing. Then arrange and rearrange the sheets of paper into a chain of events by order, either in a notebook or taped together to unfold accordion style.

- **Use folders or buckets, one each, for chronicling the stages and circumstances of your life.** One bucket or folder for early childhood, one for the elementary school years, one for adolescence; and one each for your firsts—first time on your own in a new school, job, relationship, or town. Now write down the significant events, again each on a single sheet of paper, as it comes to you. You don't have to do this necessarily in chronological order because you can sort each into the appropriate file or bucket later. The files or buckets provide the chronology, while the process gives you more freedom to simply get down the significant events and the thoughts and feelings around each.
- **Write on topics, if the idea of going through your life span doesn't fit:** anger, fear, self-esteem, body image, rejection, work, school, parents, relationships, sex, spirituality, and anything else that seems significant to you. A great resource to get you started is *The Twelve Steps: A Spiritual Journey, a Working Guide for Healing* (RPI Publishers, Revised Edition, 1994), which combines biblical principles, 12-step program wisdom, and questions to prompt self-disclosure.

As you work with any of these tools, don't worry about whether or not you're completing them perfectly. You're sure to discover important issues worthy of exploration, but miss some things too. That's okay. This is a process. You'll discover just what you need as you're able to handle it.

Look for Emotional Keys

Your thoughts and feelings, after all, hold the keys to revealing your emotional triggers. This is because it's not just identifying the significant events in your life that are important, but your responses to them.

For instance, when your family moved from a farm to the city when you were thirteen, how did you feel about your former home and your new one? Did you make new friends easily or go through a lonely period or troubling relationships? Were there positive experiences and what were they and why were they good? Were there negative experiences that stand out in your mind too? Why? What happened and how did you feel? What saved you? What was downright destructive?

> **Your thoughts and feelings, after all, hold the keys to revealing your emotional triggers.**

Or, as another example, when you were just realizing your body image, did someone make a critical comment about how you would "never look good" or thin enough or alluring? Did you take it to heart and believe it? Did you begin to put too much importance on what others thought of your appearance? Did you wear clothes styles you didn't like or feel comfortable in just because others liked or wore them? How did it leave you feeling? What happened when you dressed or got your hair cut according to styles you preferred?

When asking yourself questions like these, be intentional and mindful to describe both the actions that occurred (yours and others') as well as your feelings and thoughts (and the influencing ones around you). Nothing is petty or unimportant if it stands out in your mind. For instance, if you remember feeling hurt by your dad calling you "chubby," that is important. It's significant, if you were hurt and angry at age nine because your mom would pack your school lunch with only carrots, celery, and a half of a sandwich, while giving your brothers and sisters full sandwiches, chips, and cookies. It matters if your best friend in junior high began to leave you behind and hang out instead with more popular girls.

If you don't recall a lot of baggage in those early years, there are probably things in adolescence worth another look. Few people come through the teen years without something affecting them. How did you do socially, academically, and physically? Was it a horrible time you'd rather forget?

Don't be afraid to look at the good, the bad, and the ugly. Yes, you may find that you were forever affected by hurts, fears, anger, or bitterness. This can be hard. If it helps, write down not just what was hard but also what helped you get through this time. This identifies your strengths, the very qualities you possess that you may have forgotten or overlooked and can help you now.

In particular when looking at your thoughts and feelings, think about:

- **where you put up walls** or built bridges;
- **when you were tripped,** stopped, or stuck; and
- **where you made progress** and moved ahead.

Look at these places even more carefully and ask yourself:

- **What isolated me** or kept me from connecting with others?
- **What drew me to others** and opened up relationships?
- **When did I feel I had to be my best?** When did I feel my worst?
- **When did I feel in control?**
- **When I was out of control**, what did it look like to me?
- **What makes me feel accepted?** What makes me feel rejected?

For all these questions, think of a "for instance" and write about a specific time.

Identify Patterns

Once you see several of your responses to turning point events, begin to look for the *befores* and the *afters*: What was happening before the first time you binged? How did you feel and behave after? What caused you to binge again, what were the circumstances before the binge and events unfolding around you? How did the same circumstance affect you again after another binge, what did you do, and how did it make you feel?

The *befores* and *afters* help you find cycles. Maybe in school you were always the one picked last in gym or sports, and so every time after you had episodes of fights or withdrew from others you started seeking food as a friend. Maybe you were teased about being fat, and even though you weren't, you started to believe it, and you began to hang out on the sidelines because you would rather not be noticed at all than called out anymore. You never again took a risk in relation-

Events and circumstances can change, but the emotions triggered repeat themselves.

ships or work or even play, and you chose the company of cake instead of the company of other people.

Such cycles of behavior or feelings and thoughts help you find patterns. Events and circumstances can change, but the emotions triggered repeat themselves. You can be an adult afraid of being rejected by a possible new friend just as you felt rejected as a child in your family, and the situations with the possible friend and the family member can be totally different, but your fears are exactly the same.

The comfort, relief, and reassurance you seek can be the same too:

- Do you go into hiding?
- Do you blame others?
- Do you jump to conclusions and assume the worst?
- Are you always the victim?
- What gives you a sense of spiraling into chaos? What gives you back a sense of control?

When you think about it, most behavior and thought patterns are developed growing up. If critical outbursts were common in your home, you grew antennae, so to speak, for any kind of judgment. If you lived with an angry person who was violent, you learned to react in fear. Those reactions could go in all sorts of directions: Maybe your fear led you to avoid all conflicts, or become a peacemaker at any cost, or a people-pleaser, or to cower at anything new, or to seek all manner of protection at any cost, or become angry yourself and maybe take out your anger on others.

Everyone is different, but everyone has patterns of behavior based on things they've learned in life. Once you start seeing the patterns, you're sure to find your own emotional triggers.

Cleaning Inside Shows Outside Too

That's what Tom began to see. He could no longer deny it wasn't just his twelve-year-old response to his parents' divorce, being more on his own, and his dad's mockery that made him turn to food for comfort. It was also his fifty-year-old response to his boss's questioning if a report was thorough enough, the way he received his wife's chiding to focus when they recently painted the house, and how he felt when his increasingly independent daughters, now in their teens, chose to go off with their friends rather than stay in for conversation and a movie with dad.

The adult Tom didn't want to die when these things happened. But his response was to eat when he felt criticized by an authority figure for his ADD, or when something made him feel like "Tom the Ping-Pong," or when he was left alone by those he valued most. Tom learned his emotional triggers were situations that made him feel insecure, less-than, not-enough, flighty and unable to focus, and abandoned and isolated. The situations and even the specific go-to foods often changed, but he still was seeking to smother the emotional pain in food pleasures. He was still the twelve-year-old shutting himself away with food for consolation and escape.

He admitted no amount of willpower or diet could heal those emotional wounds. He finally agreed he would never be free to have a sane relationship with food until he dealt with the long-harbored thoughts and feelings.

So he went to work. He began to identify the wounds and sadness, call them out, and clean out his response, his negative self-talk: *I must be damaged goods, not enough to keep my parents together, so messed up my dad would call me names and not want to stay. I must not be able to focus after all since I'm Tom the Ping-Pong.*

None of those stories were true, Tom realized. He was amazingly strong and smart, overcoming many of the issues of ADD and not only getting a good job but keeping it and doing well with it for

TRIGGER TALK
Name Your Mood Triggers and Claim His Help

After you've begun this exercise of self-discovery, take time out to note succinctly what you discover are the issues you've buried, denied, tried to hide, or covered up from the turning points in your life.

For instance, as for Tom, maybe you've discovered your emotional trigger is any situation or experience that makes you feel abandoned or mocked for the way you're made. Or as for Sara, you've found you're looking for love and your emotional trigger is any situation or experience that leaves you feeling lonely or bored.

Write out your triggers so you can name them and then claim God's help to face them with faith in God and not food or anything else. There is power in naming and claiming things.

A woman who had been struggling with health issues for years discovered this when she went to Jesus for help (you can read the account in Mark 5:25–34). This woman believed even a touch from God would heal her, and since Jesus was in town she went to Him. So did a huge crowd. The woman worked her way through the people and could only grasp at the hem of Jesus's robe as He was passing by the crowd.

Even a touch will stop Jesus to help you. "Who touched Me?" He asked the crowd, even though He already knew (Mark 5:31). He didn't need the woman to tell Him it was her. But He knew she needed to voice her faith because there is power in naming your need and claiming His power to meet it.

The power was not in the act of the woman naming and claiming things, Jesus said (Mark 5:34). The power is God's and how you exercise faith in Him. So own up to your emotional triggers, own up to the need for help in overcoming them, and then move forward.

twenty-five-plus years. He was good at relationships where his parents were not—he was loving and being loved by a wonderful wife and children. He wasn't Tom the Ping-Pong but Tom the Bomb who could get things done and fast!

Tom began to rewrite these true stories of his life, replacing all the old ones others had written that he had bought into for most of his life.

When he did this, the most surprising thing happened.

Tom began losing weight. He was focused on his emotions and tackling them as much as a food plan, and he began to reach his original goal. He felt better about himself, and those around him were drawn to this vibrant, happy new Tom.

"I wouldn't have believed it," he admitted. "But it's like the saying goes: happiness really is an inside job."[1]

Talk to anyone who's focused solely on losing weight as an answer to emotional turmoil and you'll find the same thing. You can shed pounds, but the weight is not automatically replaced by happiness. Being thinner doesn't make you smarter or beautiful, efficient or loving and lovable. Getting your body in shape doesn't guarantee you'll have a new love life or more fulfilling work, more peace and less frustration. The amount of goodness you find in this world or joy you experience isn't determined by the size of your body as much as the size of your heart, the well-being of your mind, and the strength of your spirit.

> You can have remarkable weight loss and still feel unwanted, ugly, and unlovable if you haven't worked on getting your insides in shape too.

You can have remarkable weight loss and still feel unwanted, ugly, and unlovable if you haven't worked on getting your insides in shape too—because you are not just a body. You are a body, mind, and spirit, a combination of all three things. All three need tending, nourishment, exercise, and attention.

Jesus talked about this with the Pharisees, the religious folks of His day who cared more about keeping the letter of the law than the spirit of it. The Pharisees wanted to measure actions more than their effect, care more about ends or means than both. The Pharisees wanted to separate things out, just as some people today want to gauge a person's well-being by weight and appearance rather than combined health of mind, body, and spirit.

It's as ridiculous as saying the house is clean because the windows are washed. Or that you can look for love in the refrigerator, and find a friend in a bowl of ice cream that will only melt with your heart and leave you in the end.

Cleaning up the outside alone doesn't make anything fresh and new. Dealing with a part doesn't change the whole. You can clean up the outside with laws and the inside can remain unclean, full of greed and indulgence (Matthew 23:2–26). Clean the inside, though, and then the outside can be clean too.

In the same way, when you clean up what's eating you, all the fear and hurt, pain and confusion, you help yourself with how you eat. You free yourself to feel better as well as look healthier. You re-write all the old stories you had bought into of who you are and the life you must live, and you start living a new story, the true story.

Freedom was never something to be held anyway, like a refrigerator handle or a pie. Freedom starts in your heart and your mind, and it too has a taste, wonderful and more satisfying to your soul than any Turkish Delight.

SEVEN

Stinkin' Thinkin'

Every day clients walk through my office door in all shapes and sizes, ages and stages, colors and cultures, of both genders and all generations. Some are loud and talkative, others reticent and shy. Because food abuse has brought with it extra weight, these folks share common issues: obesity, self-loathing, poor body image. To a person, the thinking is the same: first blaming the body, then insulting the mind and spirit, the very self.

I'm fat.

I'm ugly.

I'm stupid.

I'm inadequate.

I will never feel, look, or be good enough.

I'm a mess, a mistake, a failure, a flop.

I'm not worthy.

The list goes on—a long train of negative thoughts, every weakness or flaw called out. Some true but most not. You know how it goes. You've probably said at least one of these things in any given day.

Clive did this when he set out to open his own accounting firm at age twenty-nine. He feared failing with his company just as he had with the food he'd abused since high school. His fears seemed to grow with his business, even though the firm was doing just fine. When he came to my office, he not only put himself down for being so fat and so afraid, he now added "being stupid" on an unwritten but very clear list of reasons for his self-loathing.

That's the way it goes. One negative thought piles into another until there's one big train wreck of a mind-set. The shame is so deep, so tangled and layered. One dig rolls into another, crashing into a pile so mangled you're trapped there.

The negative thinking becomes a habit. You pick on yourself like this all day long. You find fault with how you look, what you do, what you say, what you believe others think of you, and on and on, your thoughts looping round the track again and again, leaving a trail of wreckage, a little more of your self-confidence and worth along the way.

Even when you begin recovery, you're upset with how you ate last night and you worry about what you'll eat today. You think you should be able to conquer more in a day than is humanly possible, and you feel bad when you don't reach the outrageous expectations you've set for yourself. You think you should be a better friend, worker, husband, wife, father, mother, son, daughter—human being. You wish you could be more organized like a coworker, or tend your yard and keep your garage as neat and nice as the neighbor's. You look at your friends and think they have it all: great spouse, bright and beautiful kids, lovely home—and, in comparison, you've failed. You're flawed. You're a lost cause, damaged, no good.

You reason if you could just have a better body—be thin or at least more fit—you would be so much happier. If you had only finished school or gone for that guy, then you would be better off. If your parents had only loved you the way you needed, if you'd only been dealt a better hand, if you hadn't got the short end of the stick, if only you'd had things better . . .

If, if, if only.

THE MIND-BODY CONNECTION

So much of recovery is about changing that stinkin' thinking to healthy thinking. This is so important because your thoughts matter. Your every thought not only affects your mind, but your body and appearance too. How you carry and think of yourself, what you become in your own mind, becomes visible to others and can shape what they think of you too.

The Bible puts this well: as you think, so you are (Proverbs 23:7).

When you think you're unattractive, you become unattractive. When you believe you're a loser, you start acting like one. Notions of how no one would want to be around you begin to come true because the way you think affects how you feel, which affects how you act, which affects what you become.

See what I mean? The negative thoughts line up like cars on a long train—or, as physician and psychiatrist Daniel G. Amen sees it, like ants that crawl all over you and slip into every nook and cranny of your life.

In fact, it's what Amen calls this kind of thinking: ANTs, or Automatic Negative Thoughts. Cynical, gloomy, and complaining thoughts that seem to keep coming all by themselves, one dispiriting notion following another.[1] ANTs create a gray world full of anxiety and pessimism. If you could look into the thoughts of a depressed and fatalistic person, for instance, you would see ANTs all over the place. Regret and negativity—self-fulfilling prophecies such as "I know I won't get the job" and "They won't like me."

On the other hand when you think hopefully and positively, you create more self-promoting thoughts to help you soar and achieve.

Amen found this isn't just psychobabble. There is a mind-body connection. Thoughts have physical properties and are real, influencing every cell of your body. Every time you have a thought, your brain releases chemicals and an electrical transmission travels across your brain to its limbic center, where thoughts are signaled and registered and then corresponding moods and behavior are triggered.

When you have an angry, unkind, sad, or grumpy thought, for example, your brain releases negative chemicals that activate and heat up the deep limbic system and make your body feel bad. Muscles tense, the heart beats faster, hands start to sweat, and when the thoughts are intense you can feel dizzy and off-balance.

You're triggered to feel irritable, moody, depressed, angry, any manner of negative emotion. Which leads to more negative thoughts.

By the same token, every time you have a happy, good, hopeful, or kind thought, your brain releases chemicals to make your body feel good. The electrical transmission travels across your brain and cools your deep limbic system, bringing a sense of calm to the body. Your muscles relax, your heartbeat and breathing slow down, and your hands become dry.

I've seen the effects of good and bad thinking on the body with every client who walks through my door. The clients who haven't yet confronted their addictive behaviors live in the ANT world. They shuffle in almost apologetically, ducking slightly, cringing as if trying

TRIGGER TALK

What God Sees as Good

You've felt or seen the torture of struggling with food and the leftover self-loathing. But the mess you see is not the miracle God sees. He wants you to have His vision for how lovely and able He made you. He wants you to exchange negative thoughts for positive ones, what's untrue for His truth, bad notions for His good. Change any view of yourself as unappealing to a reminder of how we are His treasure of great worth (Matthew 4:44–46).

The next time all your self-loathing makes you feel worthless, remember: Noah was a drunk; Abraham was too old; Isaac was a daydreamer; Jacob was a liar; Leah was ugly; Joseph was abused; Moses had a stuttering problem; Gideon was afraid; Rahab was a prostitute; Samson had long hair and was a womanizer; David had an affair and was a murderer; Elijah was suicidal; Jonah ran from God; Job went bankrupt; Martha worried about everything; the Samaritan woman was divorced more to squeeze through a narrow doorway or tight turnstile. Behaving in ways that feed upon the self-loathing they confess with words and body language, they do everything they can to cover up and make their size, their very being, less noticeable. Even on warm days and in my well-heated office, they wear baggy sweaters or jackets because they're ashamed of how their arms look or they want to hide their belly or love handles. They do their best to sink into the couch and cover their midsections with the throw pillows, a purse, a magazine, or newspaper. I've met some people, standing in a foyer, trying to hide behind a potted plant or tree—anything to hide the self they've come to hate.

What a difference between the person who walks in the door

than once; Zacchaeus was too small; Paul was too religious; Timothy had an ulcer; John the Baptist ate bugs; Jeremiah and Timothy were too young; Isaiah preached naked; Naomi was a widow; Peter denied Christ; the disciples fell asleep while praying; and Lazarus was dead!

Above all else, remember you are God's workmanship, created to do good works He has long-planned for you (Ephesians 2:10).

Make this message real and work on your God vision with some ANT killer this week. On a piece of paper make two columns, with a heading on the left, MY THOUGHTS, and on the right, HIS THOUGHTS. At the end of the day, write down every time you've thought something negative (*I'm so fat, ugly, stupid*) in the left-hand column. Now, in the right-hand column, write down truths from God (*You are fearfully and wonderfully made*). Use a Bible concordance or search online for "what God thinks about us." Keep this chart in a place you can see and use to start internalizing the truth and getting rid of the ANTs.

like that and the one who has gotten rid of the ANTs. How free and confident are the people who have learned to accept themselves as they are. This has nothing to do with their size or build. The confident, self-accepting person isn't necessarily willowy, thin, and fit, with the perfect body. A person at peace with themselves and the world can be tall and large and carry their body with confidence and grace. The self-accepting person possesses a certain elegance that goes beyond size. Think singer/songwriter/actress Queen Latifah (*Chicago, Last Holiday, The Secret Life of Bees*) or late actor Michael Clarke Duncan (*The Green Mile*), whose friends called him Big Mike for his towering six-foot-four-inch stature and muscular build. They've given us pictures of how to carry even a towering frame with presence, grace, and positivity.

> Whether you lose weight quickly or it takes a long while, you can learn to accept and love, not loathe, yourself as God loves you for who you are.

You can be like that too. Whether you lose weight quickly or it takes a long while, you can learn to accept and love, not loathe, yourself as God loves you for who you are, just as He made you in word, thought, deed, dress, and shape. This is one of the gifts recovery from food abuse will give you—not just to be able to manage your emotions and meals, but to escape the obsession over what you want to fix about your body.

TAKE NO PRISONERS

This ability begins with stopping the negative thinking, period. You must take your every thought captive, the Bible says (2 Corinthians 10:5). Think on whatever is true, honorable, right, pure, lovely, and of good repute (Philippians 4:8). Dwell on what's worthy of praise.

In other words: squash the ANTs.

Don't Even Dabble

Negative thoughts are actually triggers. If you allow one, it can take you to another bad thought and another, and fairly quickly to places you don't want to go. This completely distracts you from your purposes and leads to feelings that disable you and trigger that urge to soothe yourself with food and a binge.

It happens like this: You wake up in the morning determined to do things right with food today. You've got your plan set and feel you have it all under control. By afternoon, though, a few hours till dinner, you start thinking, "Maybe I should have a little snack because I'm feeling kind of hungry." You begin worrying about it, fearing you should have eaten something else earlier so you don't have a craving now. You start to fixate on the fact you want a snack, which makes you feel guilty (*I should be stronger than this!*). All this negativity leads to a desire to comfort yourself with food. You forget all the times before when a snack led to a full-blown binge. Instead, you think about what would taste good, and then you resort to food porn. You start looking at foods you think would bring pleasure to replace how rotten you feel. You stare at the advertisement on the side of the cookie carton and imagine the pleasure of taking just one taste. Then, *boom, trigger*, you're not just looking at the outside of the container anymore. You've binged. You're staring at the bottom of the empty carton, or you're on your way to buy another one.

You could have changed everything by not dwelling on the idea of a snack. Notice I didn't say "not thinking about the idea of a snack." You can't help it if the thought registers. You're only human after all. It's the play with the stinkin' thinking that gets you into trouble, the dwelling upon it and spending time with it. You have to know you cannot entertain trigger thoughts. Period.

This works the same way when you go to a party where everyone else is raving about the dessert. You know dessert isn't an option for you. If you take your thoughts captive, and squash ideas of one taste, you'll be okay. But if you begin wondering about the dessert and how good it would taste, dwelling on it, telling yourself that reflecting on it isn't as bad as eating it, you're dangerously close to taking a taste, triggering a binge, and getting into trouble. Wonderings can turn to dabblings, and reflections to reaches: *Maybe this doesn't have too much sugar . . . maybe, if I have enough protein and veggies, I'll balance out what I've eaten in sweets . . . maybe I can indulge just this once . . .*

The "maybe" thoughts have a certain end: they will set you off and trigger another binge.

Think Free to Be Free

Squashing the ANTs, then, means inviting in positive thoughts and dwelling on the sweet taste of freedom.

Replace tempting thoughts of trigger foods with the reminder you have a food plan and it's called a *plan* because it's a course to follow, not an option. That course is a road to freedom, helping you walk away from disastrous food abuse and toward all your goals. Doesn't it feel better than being shackled to the cycle of binges that keep you isolated and shamed, behind doors with doughnuts?

Thinking about freedom and how good it tastes is what drives away the ANTs. How good it is to wake up knowing in the hours ahead you don't have to whirl around and around the decisions of what food to eat and when. You know exactly how you can manage food today, no confusion, no question, no uncertainties. How rewarding to spend time on fulfilling activities and relationships instead of obsessing over what to eat.

OBSESSION AND THE DANGER OF SWITCHING ADDICTIONS

The danger of obsessing over food is one of the most powerful parts of stinkin' thinking. You can stop the obsession with food and turn the obsession to something equally harmful: shopping, more time in front of the computer, excessive dating and pursuing multiple love interests, preoccupation with how your body looks, or sex, or a long list of other things. Just as food in itself isn't bad or good, neither are any of these pursuits—until you have a compulsion to do them—at the risk and detriment of your well-being and everything else in your life.

Switching addictions is common too, according to new studies ongoing at Harvard.[2] A 2012 roundtable of neuroscientists, surgeons, and researchers saw a number of patients who had gastric bypass surgery turn to alcohol abuse within the first year after surgery. From the research on why, the consortium of scientists and doctors believe it's because most of these people who abused food chose to work on their bodies—using a gastric band to keep them from being able to overeat—but never worked on their minds. They were food addicts, and when they could no longer physically abuse food, they turned to some other substance for the fix and obsession. There are other widely reported stories of personalities and celebrities who used gastric bypass surgery to slim down, then gained back all their weight for the same reason: the research shows it's in the mind that addictive behaviors are triggered.

This is what I see in my practice too. Clients who don't address their addictions and obsessions with one substance can stop abusing food, but will then obsess over and form an addiction to something else: shopping, alcohol, drugs, gambling, pornography, love interests, social media, television—anything that allows one to follow a compulsion for pleasure to cover some pain.

Whatever the fix is, the results are no different than switching seats on the *Titanic*. It doesn't matter which chair you choose, first class or steerage, you're going down. So when a person finds themselves obsessing over anything, secluding themselves with that fix, compulsively indulging in it at the cost of their time and schedule, relationships, pocketbook, self-worth, and very life, there is some serious stinkin' thinking to address.

Paul, thirty-nine, is an example of this. As he began recovery from a life of food abuse and loneliness, he started to obsess over losing weight and rebuilding his body. He thought a new body and attractive build would automatically translate into relationships.

Paul was doing well keeping to his food plan. But the more weight he lost and more muscle he built, the more obsessed he became with using his body to attract women. Rather than developing healthy relationships with people, he spent more and more time viewing pornography on the Internet. He began to seclude himself with porn, like he used to do with pizzas, and to masturbate several times a day.

None of this was healthy. He had simply switched giving his body pleasure with food to getting pleasure from porn and sex without relationship. Neither fix addressed all the emotional and spiritual issues that drove him to act on his triggers.

Now, in the isolation of his new obsession, he felt even more angst and shame, and absolutely no peace. He needed to stop making excuses for his new obsession and stop the very first obsessive thought that led to his ANTs. He needed to work on his emotions by addressing the triggers in his mind, no ifs, ands, or buts.

Excuses Are as Bad a Habit
as the Excess

Paul's story is only one of hundreds of powerful examples of how taking your thoughts captive—or not, as in his case—can be so powerful. The behaviors of addiction actually do begin in the brain. How you think, the choices you make, do indeed govern what you do.

The challenge, though, for anyone who has abused food or any other substance, is learning to care as much about getting the mind in shape as the body. So much of the time the myth is that recovery is about what you put in your mouth. But it's also about what you put in your mind—what you allow your thoughts to feed upon. When you start taking bad and untrue thoughts captive, you begin to dwell on what's good and right. You stop making excuses, which can be as dangerous in triggering a binge as a bunch of burgers and fries or cakes and cookies.

Check yourself here, if you've ever gone down these thought trails—each one is as much a trigger as a chocolate cream pie:

- I was sooo tired.
- Work was incredibly stressful.
- I couldn't get my kids under control.
- It was snowing and there was nothing else to do.
- It was such a beautiful sunny day I couldn't resist having some ice cream.
- I had a fight with my husband/wife.
- They brought these amazing cookies into work.
- I couldn't say no to Aunt Millie who labored to make that cake.
- Dinner was served so late, I had to eat something.
- I was driving past Dunkin' Donuts and it called my name.
- I didn't have the food I needed. I forgot to bring my lunch. I brought my lunch, but the pizza everyone else was eating looked so much better.
- It was just a little.
- It was only a Milky Way Lite.
- I have to have it in the house for my kids.
- I can't throw away the leftovers.
- I blew it earlier, so I might as well just keep on going.
- I just can't imagine never eating sugar again.
- We were watching the game together. I didn't want to be left out.
- I felt deprived.
- We were at a great restaurant.
- I paid a lot for the buffet and didn't want to waste my money.
- I was with my in-laws for the whole day.
- My boyfriend broke up with me.

- Aunt Linda died.
- I was at a party/wedding/Bat-Mitzvah/on vacation.
- It was Christmas or New Year's, Halloween, Easter, my daughter's birthday, Saturday, Sunday.
- I was bored, sad, happy, lonely, angry, frustrated, anxious, or depressed.
- I'll start tomorrow.

Most of us, at some point, have made these excuses more times than we care to admit. There's always another excuse to lead you back down the track to losing control. Then every loss of control is another reason to feel guilty, ashamed, and stuck in the same old debilitating pattern.

We need a clear resolution to give up all addictive eating and avoid anything that leads down the wrong road. It doesn't matter if Aunt Millie worked hard to make the cake, you're on vacation, or it's Christmas. You have to be clear about what's going on here. You've made excuses. You've justified this one break from the plan, which leads to another; and every break leaves you more broken, shattered, and damaged and difficult to piece together.

> **If you had a life-threatening allergy to peanuts, you would never eat peanuts just because it's Christmas.**

You have to take a hard look at how every excuse kills you a little more. The excuses are killing you, after all. Excuses can be as deadly as a bullet or poison. *Just as deadly.* Think about it. If you had a life-threatening allergy to peanuts, you would never eat peanuts just because it's Christmas. What kills you every other day will kill you on a special occasion. There are no exceptions.

If you really want to look and feel good and, better, be whole and full of life and joy, then you have to take the excuses captive in your thoughts just as you let go of excess food. Your situation has to become that apparent. You can't even think about it or toy with ins and outs.

EIGHT

It's All Peace and Love

Just as the ANTs and the excuses can be triggers, so can anxious feelings and thoughts. You can worry as much over what not to eat as you once did over what to eat or how much you ate. You can worry about how you look, and if people know what you feel so ashamed about—all the food abuse. All the fretting, stewing, and panicking can send you straight to a binge as much as a pancake or a pie can.

For years, you used food to calm those anxieties or drug and numb yourself. Now you'll see how you can arrest the anxiety without reaching for food. You might think it's going to take a lot of work and things to do, but God's way of stopping the chaos, confusion, and anxiety is to simply stop.

"Be still," He says (Psalm 46:10 NIV), "and know that I am God."

Isn't that amazing? He doesn't say work out for three more hours or start a new diet or buy more clothes as an antidote to the anxiousness of how you feel about your appearance. He says, *Stop.*

Even the words "be still," and the idea of God loving and being beside you can calm your anxious thoughts when you let them. You can be frantic in a situation where your triggers are going off—you're at a restaurant and surrounded by delicious desserts or you're on a trip far from home and there's a refrigerator stocked with candy bars in your hotel room. Your thoughts race: *Just one taste. No one will know. I know this will set me off. I know I'm on the verge of a binge here. I know this will undo all I've been doing. But . . . I can get back on track tomorrow . . .*

This is when you take God's advice. Just stop. Be still. Arrest your thoughts. Ask God to take them, and like a loving parent hushing a frightened child, God says: *All right. Let's be quiet a minute. I'm here. I'm in control. I've got you. There's a way out. I can get you out of this temptation by stilling you and allowing you to relax and refocus. Take a deep breath. Call on My strength and I'll be right here the whole time, by your side.*

As if that good advice isn't enough, God gives us more. He gives us practical steps for calming the worries: "Be anxious for nothing, but in everything by prayer and supplication with thanksgiving let your requests be made known to God. And the peace of God, which surpasses all comprehension, will guard your hearts and your minds in Christ Jesus" (Philippians 4:6–7).

It's not just wisdom. It's something you can do:

- **Pray for relief and help.** Tell God what you want and need. Bug Him about it. Call on Him again and again. Tell Him you need His guard over your mind and mouth, what you tell yourself and how you think.
- **Thank Him** for what He has done, is doing, and is going to do. Accept what is and expect what's to come. Believe He's going to do what He promises.
- **Choose to be anxious for nothing.** This is an intention. You can't help your feelings, but you can help what you do with them. Remind yourself that God says you don't need to worry about even the smallest matters, like what's for dinner or if the reception will have only cake or what to wear to the meeting, or the fact the carpet didn't get vacuumed this Saturday, or the embarrassment at the airport screening that there's a slight hole in your sock. Nor does He want you to worry about the big things. He doesn't say: *Well, if you lost your job or your child is sick, then you should be anxious.* He means don't worry about those little things *or* the big things.

SEEK PEACE AND PURSUE IT

When you're calm and relaxed, you're open to receive another part of God's great antidote for allowing your mind to help your body: peace. With peace, you can accept yourself and whatever situation comes your way. With peace, there's strength, not in your own power, but God's. With peace, you think more clearly, behave more rightly, live more freely.

Once again, however, there's an irony in how to get the peace God wants to give you.

So many of us think peace just comes to us, we wake up and have it, that we simply *are* peaceful. But does anyone go through life that way on one's own? Don't most of us, left to our own devices, roll reluctantly from bed and through life, rushing to get ready, ticking off in our heads what needs to be done, thinking through all the places we need to go and people to see and meals to plan?

Without checking in with God, without being still and letting Him do His work in us, peace won't just come, certainly not so easily. If you want peace, God says, you have to look for it: "Seek peace and pursue it" (Psalm 34:14).

Alcoholics Anonymous urges the pursuit of peace as essential in overcoming addiction. In fact, AA stresses making serenity the most important thing you practice along with sobriety. You know with your own recovery from food addiction this kind of change doesn't just happen. You must go after it.

Going after peace, however, doesn't mean working for it, because peace is God's gift. "Peace I leave with you," Jesus promised. "My peace I give to you; not as the world gives do I give to you" (John 14:27). So you don't earn peace. As with any gift, you receive it. It means you open your hands and your heart. It means you:

- **reject untrue pictures of peace.** Some people dwell on photos of super-thin, bony models or actors and actresses as inspiration for the goal they want to reach, the way they want to appear after losing weight. But those images don't bring peace and aren't true images of health. Such photos are likely retouched and reworked, varnished standards of one kind of beauty. Comparing yourself to such unrealistic and un-healthy images can only bring frustration, disappointment, and discouragement. Instead, dwell on images and stories of people who are living healthy and doing inspiring things re-gardless of their size. Your recovery isn't just about your ap-pearance but your lifestyle and whole well-being, body, mind, and spirit.

- **set boundaries and give yourself limits** with your time, endeavors, commitments, and relationships. You can't be everything to everyone all the time, and just like a checking account affords a finite amount of money, you have only so much of yourself to spend in any given day. When you're overworked and overtaxed, you're vulnerable to overeating, and that brings chaos. Giving yourself a margin, some elbow room, calms the chaos. It means you're going to say no to things that drain you. You're going to limit time on social media and electronics, including your TV and phone. You're not going to promise to meet with friends every weekend, leaving yourself without even one night to regroup. You're going to get the sleep you need so you don't fight the alarm and the day—and the vulnerability in fatigue to your temp-tations and triggers. You're going to tame your to-do list by breaking it down and noting where you make progress. When you're more reasonable about what you can humanly do in a day, you'll find the acceptance and peace to do your best and give the rest to God for another day.

- **confront and resolve problems before they can pile up**. You face issues, talk them through, and work them out with whom and what is needed. This is so different from when you used food to distract, comfort, or cover up your prob-lems (which ultimately failed). The very act, and also the consequences of overeating, only added to the upset and discord. Pursuing peace doesn't mean you absolve yourself from problems or must tie up everything with a nice bow, tuck it away, and fix it. Taking on that responsibility will only create more stress and distress. The key is in what the apostle Paul says: "If possible, so far as it depends on you, be at peace with all men" (Romans 12:18). *If possible. So far as it depends on you.* You cannot control everything. You don't create the peace. God gives it. So you do what you can do, as far as it depends on you, to face things, build bridges, stay positive, and keep moving forward no matter what others do. People will disappoint, frustrate, and hurt you; you're sure to experience disappointments, abandonment, insecurity, loss, and anger. You can't control what they do, but you can control your reactions and thoughts toward them. You can face what's been done and then do what you can and give the rest to God. This means trying not to exert all your energy on knowing how God will handle things and instead accepting that He will. This is freeing in itself. Instead of letting yourself feel powerless over the wrongdoings of others, you can focus on what you can do, even if the fault belongs to someone else, and let everything else go. Forgiveness, as you've learned, isn't what you do for others anyway. It's what you do for yourself.

- **say no to worrying.** This goes along with squashing the ANTs. You must confront yourself when you start to worry. Think of putting your worries in a box and handing the box to God. You can't change or resolve anything with your worries, and as with ANTs, one worry leads to another that only invades your soul and undoes you. So this is where you have to be intentional and aggressive. You have to take the anxious thoughts captive. One way to do this is to replace a worry with a wonder. Think not on the storm but on how our awesome God can get you through to the other side.

So, in looking at what pursuing peace means, do you notice all these verbs? You reject, set, give, contain, confront, resolve, and say *no*. The peace that then comes to you will be beyond what you could puzzle out or make happen on your own. God says it "surpasses all comprehension" (Philippians 4:7). Instead of being tangled up in the worries and whys, in unrest and conflict, you can follow a positive path, do what you know to be right, let God handle the rest, and be free. Your heart and mind can be at peace—and that will transform how you carry yourself and eventually your very body shape and size too.

Learn to Love Your Body

It's what you're longing for, isn't it? You want all the work of recovery you're doing on the inside to show on the outside. You want to see results in your body. That's why making peace with your body may be the final frontier of recovery from food abuse. Your body image may have driven you to abuse food to begin with, and now it's one of the ways, misguidedly, you may be tempted to measure the success of your recovery.

When I'm recovered, you think, *I'll be thin*. But that's not necessarily true. As you stop the binges and begin eating healthy, you're sure to become stronger and healthier, but your overall weight loss goal may happen easily and quickly or it may take time. That's okay. Size and weight aren't the measures of your success anyway. Success in recovery means you are living free in mind, body, and spirit, whatever the size or shape of each of those parts of you.

So how do you love who you are now?

Change Your Thinking to What's True
Start by looking away from the mirror and stick to your food plan no matter what, no matter if you're not hungry or if you think you're fat. It's easy to think less food consumed will mean less weight and depriving yourself of food is the antidote to getting into shape. But you

know it's not true. It's why diets don't work. Thinking *less food means less weight* actually works in reverse. Depriving yourself only makes you miserable, vulnerable, hungry, and prone to triggers and overeating. Spending more money on self-help gadgets and services won't address the addictive behavior.

So you need to take captive those untrue thoughts that more diet and exercise are the answers. Replace what's untrue with what's true: *My food plan is helping me stay the course and staying the course will show up inside and outside over time. What I do now will make a difference now.*

Change Your Mind to the Today Channel

The idea of *now* is important. When the negative thoughts start, you need to change the channel in your mind from thinking on tomorrow to today. You can't control tomorrow or even know what will happen there. You can control this moment.

When you think so much on tomorrow, you're totally wasting time anyway. You're not changing anything except your self-esteem and your mind-body connection, where you draw out all those self-deflating reactions. No amount of self-abuse will fix your body. So to change your body, change your mind. Stop dwelling on what you think you are (weak, fat, flawed, disappointing), and think upon what you are with God's help: stronger, beautiful, bold, whole.

> No amount of self-abuse will fix your body. So to change your body, change your mind.

As you practice good thinking about yourself, you stay fixed on what's doable, what makes you wonderful. All those good thoughts build up your esteem, stature, and sense of empowerment. This can translate into you sitting straighter, walking taller, and feeling full of grace—because you are.

God loves all of you just as you are, even as He's healing you and working with you through recovery, not just after. There's a beautiful expression of this in the book *Honoring the Body*: "Whenever Jesus patted mud into the eyes of someone who could not see, or touched a leper or sat at the bedside of the sick and dying, he taught how God sees and honors the body."[1] God doesn't just honor the newborn body or the perfectly preserved one. He honors the dust He makes into the

TRIGGER TALK

Self-Care: A Tool for Transformation

When you've been in an addictive cycle, using food or anything else to answer your problems and feed your needs, you're probably not good at self-care. Yet self-care is part of the antidote for changing bad habits to good ones.

So what are your self-care habits? Your eating habits will be a major focus as you work on sticking to a healthy food plan. But what about rest, relaxation, your work-play balance, relationships that buoy you, stress relief, dental and vision checkups, and workouts? On paper, look at and leverage your:

- **Rituals.** What helps you start and end your day? A cup of coffee and shower every morning? Clean pajamas and a bit of reading in bed every night? If your life is a blur of flopping in and out of bed, sometimes in the clothes worn all day or with a project on your laptop at your bedside, you'll find simply practicing some rituals to help you gear up and wind down will bring peace into your life. Lisa, sixty-one, begins her mornings reading the Psalms for thirty minutes to fill her soul. Kent, forty-three, meets a mentor for breakfast every Saturday to sort out the week past and the one ahead. Cynthia, thirty-one, reads another chapter in a storybook to her children each evening to stay connected to them and to her own sense of childlike wonder and imagination. Gordon, thirty-nine, takes the dog for a long walk every evening to leave behind stress. Write down the body, the dust to which it returns, and all the states of the body in between: the sick and ailing and imperfect and, yes, the fat. He honors what the body is and what it can become, and the mind and spirit it contains.

> things you do every day that feed your body, mind, and spirit. How can you celebrate their place in your life more?
>
> - **Lifestyle shifts.** There may be things other than your food plan and eating behaviors that need shifting in your life. For instance, do you work at home or bring work home? Are you always at work? Do you have working hours that clearly begin and end? Do you keep a Sabbath day of rest each week? What limits and boundaries can you set on when you work and play, when you rest and recreate? Keep an activity journal for one week to look at where you can make clearer boundaries, where to shift your lifestyle to allow you to function better, with more energy and peace.
> - **Ability to make it easier.** How can you give yourself what you need to be your best without struggle? If bubble baths on Friday nights help you wash away the stress of the week, can you keep the bubble bath tubside? If outdoor walks in the fresh air help you clear your head and make you feel good with all those endorphins, can you keep walking shoes and a jacket by the door? If reading about extraordinary accomplishments inspires you to think creatively and do better work, can you find a book on such things to read at lunch each day? List fifteen things or situations and connections that make you feel cared for, nourished, and inspired. How can you build at least four of them into this week?

Change What You Tell Your Body

One way to love you as God loves you is to praise Him for what is, every part of you, even the parts you've long loathed. You don't just change your feelings for yourself with the wave of a wand or a fork. You begin the conversation with praise for God's gifts, all the parts of your body you appreciate and the parts you wish were somehow different or better, and this leads to accepting the whole of you.

The book *When Women Stop Hating Their Bodies* gives a helpful exercise for starters.[2] Have a dialogue with the part of your body you loathe most. Tell it exactly how you feel, imagine what it might say in reply, and make apology for loathing it. For example, maybe you loathe your belly. But your stomach helps you stay alive by digesting the food you do need to eat. You've punished your stomach when you were overeating, and still it did its job and more by providing you with a cushion for your spouse or kids to snuggle and rest their heads against. (Who wants to cuddle a bony belly anyway?) You may not love your stomach, but there are positive ways of viewing the same unloved area.

You'll be surprised by the feelings you're able to express to a part of your body you've hated. The exercise may be so cathartic and illuminating, you start with one part and then address others significantly good or bad to you. This helps you make amends to the parts of your body you've thought of so meanly and hatefully. Here's how I talked to my stomach, imagining its reply to me:

> **Me:** I think you're fat and ugly. I've hated you since I was young. I wish you were flat like my friends' bellies. It makes me angry no matter how hard I try, you're still always there sticking out, making me look fat, making clothing look bad on me.
>
> **My Belly:** You're so mean to me. You hurt my feelings. I had no idea you feel the way you do. Every day I'm here for you to help you digest your food so you can live. Imagine what it would be like if I wasn't here. You would be very sick. By the way, I'm the place your babies grow.

Me: I know all of that, and, of course, you make some good points, but why can't you do all of those functional things and also look better? There are lots of people who have bellies that digest food and hold babies but are not so ugly.

My Belly: Ouch! You keep calling me ugly and it really hurts! I can't really fix the way I look. It's the way I was made. It sure would be nice if you could just accept me the way I am. What have I ever done to deserve this abuse from you?

Me: Okay, I don't want to hurt you. You're just really difficult to deal with. I'm sorry for how I feel. I didn't mean to make you feel bad.

My Belly: Well, do you think you would be willing to try to be more accepting of me, a little nicer to me? It's not like your constant criticism makes me look any better.

Me: You're right. Yes, I'll work on it. I don't want to make you feel bad. Complaining doesn't help matters, does it? I'm sorry for hurting you with all of these years of verbal abuse.

See how an exercise like this can let you love all of who you are right now? There are negative things like this that you tell yourself, and parts of your body, every day. Yet you can control the conversation and drive away the ANTs. You can replace self-denigrating thoughts with self-promoting ideas like how good it is you have a chance to change and a body that can get stronger.

LIVE ABOVE YOUR CIRCUMSTANCES

Coming to terms with food addiction is not easy. No one wants to have to eat differently than everyone else or to explain their new eating habits to friends, family, or nosy people. It's so easy to feel sorry for ourselves and keep wondering: *Why me? Why do I have this stupid problem?* It's so easy to stay stuck in our circumstances by continuing the stinkin' thinking of *I can't, I'm not, I'm a failure.*

It only wastes time.

Instead, begin living more richly, abundantly, and free starting right now by allowing God to do what He promises: to transform us by the renewing of our minds (Romans 12:2).

We allow God to work that transformation when we choose to think: *Why* not *live in recovery? Why not live abundantly in spite of a past of food abuse—despite wishes for thinner thighs and a flatter stomach, or the comparisons to what the world says is beautiful, or whether those standards come from Hollywood or cultures where feet are bound and ears are stretched.*

The Bible calls this living above our circumstances.[3] Things can be hard, you can think you're not good enough or smart enough or thin enough or beautiful enough or simply enough. God says: *Enough! Be patient. Strengthen your heart. Endure. Pray. Be cheerful. I'm with you and for you, and can bring about all you pray for and move toward.*[4]

The Lord is full of compassion and mercy, and waits to raise us from whatever ails us.[5] Remember the way of stinkin' thinking? The diatribe: *I'm fat and ugly and stupid? I'm not worthy?* Strike those thoughts from your mind. God in His mercy lavishes riches on us. He cares about all of us. He doesn't want us hating ourselves and overeating any more than He wants us thin and still thinking badly of ourselves. He says:

You're strong.
You're beautiful.
You're capable.
You're more than enough.
You will always be wonderful just as you are.
You're My miracle, My wonder, My wow.
You are worthy.
I gave everything for you.

Renew your mind on what He promises and how He sees you because He is true and He wants to transform all of you—not just your body, but your body and your mind and your spirit.

NINE

Walking the Minefield

Before going into battle, Roman generals would tell anyone in for the fight, "Gird your loins!" The idea was to hike up your long tunic, whether it was ankle- or knee-length, and pull the back of the skirt through your legs to tie it with the front. This secured your backside, unhindered your legs, and kept you from tripping and taking a hit. Girding your loins freed you not only to do battle but to overcome.

I'm not a Roman general, but I can tell you now's the time to gird your loins.

You've learned how to tell the difference between emotional and physical hunger, and you've learned to be aware of your negative— and positive—thinking patterns. Those skills have your back. They'll help you stay on your feet. Now, to keep from tripping up, you've got to secure yourself one more way: you've got to address the enemy that's so difficult to fight because you can count on it to come at you with a fury, in full force, as dangerous as a bag of potato chips or creamy milkshake. Only it's stealthy, often in disguise, difficult to see.

It's because this enemy comes from within. I'm talking about the ways you've learned to react to a difficult person or situation that can trip you up—the behavior that probably drove you to binge to begin with. Except now you've removed go-to foods as a coping mechanism, so the unhealthy ways of reacting can trigger you with a vengeance to want to go back to food again for comfort. This enemy, your learned behaviors, can stop and trip you back into a mad cycle of behaviors just as you had with food.

Carol discovered this. At thirty-nine, she began to face her food and emotional triggers and change inside and out. Friends told her how much more energetic she seemed. "Glowing," her sister said, commenting on how well Carol was eating without overeating or binges. A real breakthrough. Carol did seem to change shape right before everyone's eyes. The pounds melted away. Because she wasn't thinking about food all the time or spending so much energy, so many hours trying to hide her binges, she had reserves for things she'd only talked or dreamed about for years: starting a new gardening business, landscaping her property. She was beginning to make things happen. Everything seemed more beautiful; so much was going right.

Then Carol began to have troubles with her marriage. She began to feel weighed down again—only this time with frustrations, worries, and hurt rather than pounds and fat.

Carol's husband, Gary, had always indulged in some unhealthy behavior. It was one of the things that triggered Carol to reach for food as the mythical fix. Gary often worked long hours and missed supper and events they'd planned on together without even a call ahead or an "I'm sorry" afterward. He'd go on drinking binges with his buddies and lock himself away for hours in their home's study.

But now Gary wasn't just indulging in occasional destructive behavior. He was pursuing it full tilt.

"I never see him," Carol said. "He's . . ." She floundered for words. "He's lost to me. Both of us have to be at work early in the morning, so there's no time to talk in the rush to get the kids to school and ourselves out the door. Then Gary doesn't come home till late, late, late. I've tried waiting him out, but he's usually drunk so there's not much point. Weekends, he goes out with his buddies earlier and comes home later. When he is home, he shuts himself away for longer periods of time."

Carol discovered why in the evidence on their home office computer. "Porn," she said. "I think Gary's as addicted to pornography now as I was to food, and he's not remotely interested in changing."

Carol admitted she was struggling to cope. A husband unwilling to work on his addictions made her want to eat her way through hers. But she liked the changes in her own self too much to fall back into the mad overeating cycle again. So, instead, she tried giving Gary the silent treatment and distancing herself emotionally the little time they were in the same room together. When that didn't work, she compensated for all his needs more than her own, from making sure his clothes were clean for work and fixing all their meals to balancing the checkbook and being loving in bed even if she wasn't in the mood. Then she tried evoking his sympathy and that of everyone around them.

None of this changed Gary and only frustrated Carol. The isolation freed him and left her feeling more alone. The caretaking enabled him and exhausted her. Playing victim alienated Gary and sent Carol into a downward spiral of self-pity. All the while, her feelings of loneliness and fatigue triggered her to want food for comfort again.

By the time she admitted this in my office, the battle was fully raging: Gary was pursuing his addictions as hard as Carol struggled to keep in check her own addictions in eating, isolating, caretaking, and behaving from a victim mentality. She also experienced a new depth of sadness and depression.

What's in Your Minefield?

You may find you're in such a behavior battle too. Everyone reacts at some time, often without realizing, in ways that are manipulative, unhealthy, and ultimately self-destructive. Just as there are go-to foods, we have these go-to reactions—reactions familiar to us, that worked for us in the past and have become habit. We rely on them to give us, if even for a moment, what we're looking for: control and, for Carol, relief, release, escape, pleasure to replace pain, and the list goes on.

It's like walking a minefield.

Before Diana, Princess of Wales, walked the minefields of Angola and Bosnia in 1997, more than eight hundred people died every month from stepping on a land mine left over from war.[1] Those not killed outright (another twelve hundred people a month), lost limbs and suffered handicapping injuries. Upon her visit with the British Red Cross, more than five thousand land mines were cleared from one village alone. But an estimated fifteen million remained, buried, triggered by the simple footstep of villagers crossing a field or walking down a hill.

TRIGGER TALK

Behaving Gladly

When someone you love is working through behavior battles, you'll be tempted to fight a few of your own for understanding, empathy, and patience. If you haven't already been the brunt of behavior flare-ups like the avoidance or dependency, the micro-managing or drama, you will be now. So, more important than ever, remind yourself and the one you love to:

- **Keep taking care of yourself.** Living with any amount of difficulty or challenge is exhausting. You need time, energy, space, and reserves of your own. When you're tempted to brood on the difficult situation or person, think instead of one renewing thing to do for yourself: a walk to tap into your endorphins and breathe fresh air; time out for encouragement from a friend; an hour of focusing on something beautiful such as a book, art, poem, or garden; or people-watching in the city square.

- **Avoid self-blame.** Intentionally remind yourself you can't control others' decisions. You can't force someone else to change. Repeat to yourself as a prayer, a meditation: *I give to You, O God, the things out of my control. I receive, O God, Your mercy and strength.*

"The mine is a stealthy killer," Diana said in a speech that drew worldwide attention.[2] "Long after the conflict is ended, its innocent victims die or are wounded singly, in countries of which we hear little. Their lonely fate is never reported. The world, with its many other preoccupations, remains largely unmoved."

What a picture of how you can focus on stopping your food triggers and other missteps that keep you right there on the battlefield. Beneath the surface everyone has ways, some healthy, some not, of

- **Ask for help.** Talk to a professional. Go to a support group such as Al-Anon [online at http://www.al-anon.alateen .org/] for spouses, families, and friends of alcoholics. So many of the principles in addiction can help whenever there's a loss of control (even the occasional) with food or behavior.
- **Remove yourself from the influence.** Don't argue or try to reason with someone in the midst of a binge or behavior battle. When someone's under the influence of a habit, you won't make any progress. Rather, say, "Let's talk later," and, "I love you and will be here for you when you can work through this with me."
- **Stay positive. If that's too much, at least avoid the negative**, which can fuel feelings of guilt and push someone to keep behaving in unhealthy ways. This doesn't mean turning on the sunshine, becoming perky. It does mean reminding yourself and the one you love: *This moment, this situation will pass. Things will look and feel different on the other side. There is hope. You will change or the situation will change. They will. You can move forward. You can transform.*

reacting to difficulties that can be destructive. Our culture tells us to take our frustrations out with a fork or a spoon, a carton of ice cream or order of fast food—a land mine of triggers waiting to set off the life bombs to make us lose parts of ourselves: a relationship, a dream, a goal. All the while, there are other land mines triggering the urge to binge or overeat.

Finding and dealing with those trigger behaviors is the challenge. We don't naturally see them, sometimes because we feel ashamed, other times because of disbelief, and often because we don't know what to look for in how we act. But the pursuit, the search, is what restores our whole selves—mind, body, and spirit. Or, as Jesus put it in Luke 11:34 (NIV), "When your eyes are healthy, your whole body also is full of light."

Think about this for a minute. What are your go-to reactions when you're frustrated? Or hurt? Angry? Disappointed? Do you even know how you typically react to difficulties, or if your behavior is triggering you to become vulnerable once again to a binge or going back into the cycle of losing control with food? Take a closer look.

Isolation and Avoidance

Whether you've lost control with food once in a while or in regular ways that ruin your life, you've learned all about isolation. You know how to hide the episodes and the evidence. You've felt ashamed of the overeating and your body, so you've binged in secret and suffered in silence. When the going gets tough, you pull away and shut yourself off.

Just as with food, shutting down, avoiding the truth, and not facing the issues or retreating from them doesn't solve a thing.

Now you're beginning to manage the eating issues. But, like Carol, other issues are cropping up or looming larger. Maybe you've been noticed at work and handed some challenging projects. You are feeling overwhelmed and want to delegate away the troublesome tasks. That's processing, though, not problem-solving. Or maybe your ten-year-old is getting into trouble at school and defying you at home, taking off with the neighbor kids without a word on his whereabouts for hours at a time. You're frustrated but can't face the fight you are sure he'll put up—what would you do if he simply refuses to mind? So you retreat and skirt around confrontation. You let him lock himself away in his room or in front of the computer for hours. You're not stepping up as a parent now. You're becoming a pushover.

In either situation, just as with food, shutting down, avoiding the truth, and not facing the issues or retreating from them doesn't solve a thing. The problems just grow. What arrests the isolation and avoidance triggers is to engage and get involved, not absolve yourself or go absent.

Control

Like Ted, you may react to anything uncertain, worrisome, or difficult by trying to control it. Now forty, Ted spent his childhood floating between the two households of separated parents, each trying to blend a new family. He yearned to control something, anything, everything because so much kept changing: where he lived and went to school, who got along with whom, and a dozen other things. For years, the one thing he could count on, take charge of, and find within his grasp most of the time was food. Well before his teens, he ordered pizzas and pasta for delivery. Placing the order gave him the empowerment he wasn't getting anywhere else. He called, the food came. *Control.* At least until eating all the made-for-delivery food got out of control.

After nearly twenty years of bingeing, Ted wanted fitness and freedom. As he learned to control his eating, though, other things seemed to spin beyond his grasp. He reacted as he had with food, grabbing for as much as he could get. He micromanaged his team at work to the point of ordering "no more drinking coffee in meetings." He bossed his college-age son on how to mow the lawn in diagonals. He told his wife where to gas up the car, how to order her morning so they wouldn't be late for church, which way to put the toilet paper on the roll, and what shoes (those easy slip-ons) to wear on their evening walk. He thought this would give him some certainties: staff wouldn't waste time on coffee runs, his son would better manicure the lawn, and his wife could save time fueling up the car and getting ready for church and their walk. (Who knows what the toilet paper issue was about—don't most couples jockey for control of that one?!)

When Ted's staff balked, his son mutinied from yard duty, and his wife refused to walk with him (and talk, at one point), Ted was triggered to order a few pizzas and some pasta again. It seemed an order he could control. He knew what he'd get and it would be satisfying . . . for a moment. But the outcome was no longer what he wanted.

He needed as much freedom from the madness of trying to manipulate what might, could, and would happen in this life as he needed from his Italian-food trigger. There were no assurances for what would come his way, but there were in how he could react. He began to ask himself every time the urge to control something reared its ugly head: *Does this really matter?*

He started to see the lawn looked pretty good as it had been mowed by his son, who hadn't balked or needed reminding of the chore for years, something to appreciate more. At work, Ted chose to be grateful the job got done whether his staff drank their coffee in meetings or not. As for the shoes his wife chose to wear on their walks? It didn't affect him, nor did whether the toilet paper faced up or down, or if the car got fueled up where he suggested. He learned to be grateful, and he saw it was better to get to church, period, as opposed to getting there not at all or angry.

One of the principles Alcoholics Anonymous uses is what helped Ted: peace matters more than control, because you're not ultimately in control anyway. God is. You can't make the grass grow or not, nor your employees like caffeine or not. You can't make your wife love you enough to walk with you in the evening. You can do what you can to be a wise dad, fair boss, loving husband, mindful eater, and peace-loving and noncontrolling person. Serenity will taste better, longer, than pasta, pizza, or pseudo control.

Drama Kings and Queens

Cammy, twenty-six, used to binge because she felt so lonely and craved attention. She had meltdowns with food behind a closed door, and with her friends, over feeling fat and not having a boyfriend . . . or someone treating her wrong or judging her, or a dozen other things. For Cammy, nothing was small. Everything was major. A friend ran late for their appointment at a coffee shop. Big deal. The boss needed her to put in a little overtime with everyone else for an upcoming merger of the company. Huge problem. Her parents canceled the family ski trip to celebrate Christmas at home. Major issue.

Everything had to be a big production, from Cammy's binge runs through several different fast-food joints (after which she'd park in a secluded place and down it all), to getting mad or sad and running the gamut of extremes in emotions to get the attention she wanted on issues. People responded to her when she lost control, created a scene, or forced their emotional hands by erupting in anger or ranting or bursting into tears or going on and on in exuberance.

So when Cammy began to work on what triggered her to eat, she saw that her drama *du jour* and the prima-donna behavior over other things was triggering her as much as certain foods—and ruining her relationships. Instead of hiding to eat, she was stealing away for attention, wanting friends and family to chase her down for being upset and clamor to help or make amends.

What she really wanted, though, was companionship and friendship, love and time, not their remedies and ill will in the end—and there was always an end to these relationships. Friends and family got fed up with Cammy's antics and the angst.

She needed a drama-queen plan: some dos and don'ts for situations where she used to wig out, then binge on attention. She needed to learn how to be honest about what she wasn't getting, and accept people's help instead of keeping them at arm's length so they would worry over her.

Caretaking

This was the behavior that triggered Carol most, and I see it often with clients who come to me for help with overeating. Take away the food, and it's easy to binge on taking care of others instead of other areas of yourself, like your spirit and emotions. Carol always circled back to the notion, after the isolation and victim modes didn't work to change Gary, that she should make up somehow for what she obviously lacked that drove him to his own unhealthy behavior. So she fussed over him, tended to his needs while ignoring her own, and became hypervigilant in their children's lives, going to every soccer game and school event, hovering and helping on every piece of homework. She did the same with church events too. Because Gary was absent, Carol tried to make up for it. She tried to be everywhere and everything. She binged on caretaking and became just as miserable with that as she had with the food.

But Gary's actions were his choices, not Carol's doing. Giving more to him and trying to make up for him with their children wasn't the solution, just part of the problem.

This is what's tricky about caretaking. It looks great. Everyone likes it. You believe caring for others is good and godly. But how do you know when you're caring for the right reasons or when you're doing it because it's the only way you know how to relate? How do you know when you're hiding behind caring for others because it's easier to think of them than to let anyone care for you? How do you know if you're saying yes to what others need because you don't have the confidence or esteem to say no and set boundaries? Are you sure you aren't trying to solve someone else's problems so you can avoid going to work on your own?

Once again, we are getting honest with ourselves. There is no way to perfectly answer these questions. The very same caring behavior is sometimes good and other times it is codependency in action.

We can pay more attention and develop more awareness about our caring behaviors. We can learn to listen inside and see if we are doing things for reasons of guilt, fear, or inadequacy. What are our motives? We try to make better choices when we consider our actions.

Depending Too Much on Others

Not being able to say exactly what you need and feel can be the root of a lot of other unhealthy behaviors that trigger you to reach for food. Monica, fifty-six, used to binge because sweets numbed the pain for a moment of being involved with a man who was hostile and abusive.

She fell in love with him practically upon first sight when they met in their forties and quickly began to do whatever she could to keep him happy. She was so afraid of losing him and being alone that she put up with severe verbal assaults and occasional physical threats. She held on to him for the little bit of loving she got between attacks, which is what her relationship with sweets was like too. She ate for the moments of pleasure between all the craziness of the binges and pain of adding on pounds.

When she took away the food, she realized the folly of dependency. She needed to put her faith in the right things. She didn't need to binge to feel full or have a boyfriend to be happy. In fact, her codependence on him would keep triggering her to want to eat, like it had in the beginning.

You might be too dependent on someone or something in less dramatic ways. Maybe at work you put in way more hours, keeping up on e-correspondence till two and three a.m. and going back at it at six a.m., volunteering for every new project and extra tasks because you think this makes you indispensable. Maybe you can't go anywhere on your own and call on another friend incessantly. Maybe instead of ever saying what you like, you let others make the choice of the restaurant, the movie, the way to spend the day.

Here is where you take small steps to break the dependency. You learn to say no and choose what's good for you instead of always what's good for someone else at your cost. You learn to fight for yourself and speak up for yourself, instead of passively accepting whatever is chosen for you.

So did you see yourself in these character traits? Identify your go-to reactions? Knowing is half the battle—now you're ready to change.

TEN

Tackling the Trigger Strongholds

Now you're at the heart of the battle. This is the most terrifying place. For years you've avoided it. You've tried ducking, running and stealing away, distracting yourself and denying what's really eating you. But the battle is real, as is the enemy who's left you hurt, empty, and reaching for food. At the stronghold, you have to take down the enemy, which is your deepest hurts and your greatest fears, or you'll continue to cycle in grief, depression, and rage left unresolved.

Sound dramatic?

It is. But this place of battle doesn't always show up that way. Sometimes it's clear you have a food addiction and when food is removed you binge on behavior, like Ted who described himself as becoming "a control freak," or Carol, who cycled through serious bouts of depression. Other times this place is foggier, murky and shadowed. You don't see the enemy as . . . an enemy, more just the daily things we deal with in our human nature. For instance, maybe you lose control with food just now and then. Maybe you have a tendency to caretake, but not to the extent that you've completely neglected yourself. Maybe once in a while, you become melancholy or experience the blues. Doesn't everyone?

Even if the issues at your stronghold aren't ruining your life, they still can throw you out of whack on occasion and make you vulnerable to whatever promises a quick escape or relief. You can live more fully and freely when you conquer those deepest hurts and greatest fears—and everyone has some of both.

Rachel, twenty-one, realized this when we set to work on what had made her binge since her teens. She stopped eating the sugary foods that triggered her and talked about how they became part of her life to begin with, how she would steal away with an entire batch of cookie dough or a whole cake to eat as an escape from her mother's criticisms. The food numbed the deep resentment she felt toward her mom, whose voice still rang in Rachel's mind: *Why do you even try? You need a more attractive hairstyle. That makes you look even fatter. Why do you walk like that? Can't you sit up straight for once, or are you just too out of shape?* Rachel felt so much rage toward her mom her anger erupted over small things, like a friend suggesting a new style of shoes on a shopping trip. Rachel took the notion as criticism and lashed out against what was never meant that way at all.

WHAT ARE YOUR STRONGHOLDS?

In the behavior battle, do you know your greatest fear, hurt, or unmet need? You can overcome them, but you may have only suspected some of your issues and never before named them outright. There's a power in such identification, and here are the common strongholds clients tell me can trigger abuses of food and behavior.

Anger

It's so easy to get mad over a dozen little things any given day. You get an electric bill that seems too high. The salad you ordered at the restaurant doesn't seem fresh enough and took forever to arrive at your table. Someone cuts you off driving to work . . . or in the elevator . . . or in trying to park the car. A peer digs at your ability as a professional or as a parent. Someone stands too close, invades your personal space, talks over you and interrupts, shuts down an idea. Your wallet gets stolen or flowers get picked from your front yard or one friend slanders another. People seem to push your buttons all day long. How much control do you have over those buttons anyway? Is there some seething undercurrent inside you?

It's okay, natural even, to feel angry when you're wronged or hurt. Abuse, unfairness, world affairs, traffic, stupidity, neglect—each of these things can trigger anger. Jesus felt angry too.

What to do with those feelings is where to fight the battle. Eating with a vengeance doesn't help. Nor does stuffing anger until it either implodes, resulting in everything from unease and unrest to anxiousness and depression, or erupts into damaging relationships and maybe property (ever broken a pencil, slammed a book onto a tabletop, or dropped something in anger?).

Anger is often a secondary emotion to cover some of the other strongholds we'll look at here, particularly what triggered Rachel's food abuse and anger toward her mom.

Resentment

The moment you allow negative feelings to go unresolved is the moment resentment begins to take root and grow, even without tending. In fact, when it comes to addiction (whether the addiction is to food or alcohol or some other substance) or abuse (just a binge, just an out-of-control episode of eating now and then), resentment is the number one reason for causing you to reach for something numbing. The *Alcoholics Anonymous Big Book* says resentment kills more alcoholics than anything else.[1]

This is because resentment acts like poison in the soul. It can come from understandable reasons like abuse, neglect, or unfairness. But you choose whether to give it room to root and grow. If you do, it doesn't just spread, but festers and rots your hopes, dreams, and ability to trust and believe. It hurts you more than the person or situation that caused it by making you its

> **Resentment is the number one reason for causing you to reach for something numbing.**

slave. It does other damage too—and this is talked about regularly in addiction model discussions, by support groups, and in counselors' offices:

- **absorbs** your digestion
- **creates** grief
- **saps** your energy
- **robs** your peace of mind
- **erodes pleasure** in work
- **kills** your sense of goodwill
- **invades** your thinking by keeping your attention fixed on the person or situation you resent
- **interrupts** your sleep
- **influences** your speech and tone of voice
- **can trigger you** to take medicine for all this

Resentment can also lead to the next stronghold.

Depression

This one is a tail-chaser. Have you abused food because you're depressed, or are you depressed because you've abused food? Have you cycled into caretaking or playing the victim because you feel hopeless, or do you feel hopeless because you've behaved this way? Which came first? Does it matter, when you can't really resolve one without addressing the other?

Depression can be so debilitating, and for the person triggered by food it can bring on extra grief. Eating certain foods, like sugar with its energizing properties, brings some relief from the experience of cardboard lifelessness. But giving in to your trigger foods and stuffing your sorrows with sweets doesn't bring freedom and only triggers both the bingeing and certain behavior triggers, especially isolation and avoidance, which in turn feed the depression. You can feel hurt and sad and, like a wounded animal, steal away in pain. At first, the isolation seems soothing. Then the aloneness deepens. You don't feel worthy of company, or wanted, or needed. The longer you keep to yourself, the more you disengage from life, and the greater the hold of the depression. So you stay isolated and depressed, and you avoid the chance of more hurt—and healing.

Fear

Most people wrestle with this stronghold, and it can be at the root of all the others, because our list of fears is long and deep and drives so much of what we do or keep from doing. We fear failure, success (*Can I keep it up?!*), intimacy, being alone, sickness, hurt, medicines, surgery, death, the unknown, change, the status quo, people, animals, creepy crawly things, birds, the dark, the burning sun, heights, the ocean, the desert, flying, falling, and so on. It's probably because our fears are so many and so great that in the Bible God and His messengers tell us more than 366 times (at least once for every day in the year): *Fear not.*

We need the daily reminder because of how fear stops us, keeps us from forming healthy relationships, expressing love, speaking up, and setting boundaries, each a key issue for anyone who's wrestled with food. We need the reminder because fear also starts us up and triggers us—to binge for comfort; isolate and avoid, or retreat, for protection; and caretake or create drama as distraction. These lists go on as well. So what are we to do?

Let It Begin with Me

Once you see strongholds like anger, resentment, depression, and fear buried in your emotional minefield, you can't just walk away.

When I broached this with Rachel, she bristled. "Facing your mother and mending your relationship will defuse the resentment and help you move forward," I explained.

"This is so unfair!" she railed. "Why am I the one who has to fix this? She's the one who pushed me into bingeing and depression. She's the one who berated me till I knew I would never measure up, never could be good enough. I'm the one wounded."

Exactly.

When you realize you're the one losing parts of yourself on the minefield—your confidence, your peace, your hope—you need the help first. Thousands of people lost limbs and lives before Princess Diana and the British Red Cross arrived on the minefields of Angola. The ones who planted the mines had moved on already. The ones who wound and hurt us, whether intentionally or not, may never return to see our peril. Sad as it is, they may never care.

> We, who are wounded, care not because the enemy deserves a mended relationship, but because we deserve to heal.

We who are wounded care, not because the enemy deserves a mended relationship, but because we deserve to heal.

We begin, like Princess Diana, with a willingness to shine light on the minefield, to see what's there. Then we go forward toward freedom from the land mines of grief, anger, depression, and bitterness, and, following the example in the prayer of St. Francis of Assisi,[2] take the first step toward peace:

Lord, make me an instrument of Your peace;
where there is hatred, let me sow love;
where there is injury, pardon;
where there is doubt, faith;
where there is despair, hope;
where there is darkness, light;
where there is sadness, joy.

O divine Master, grant that I may not so much seek
to be consoled as to console;
to be understood, as to understand;
to be loved, as to love;
for it is in giving that we receive;
it is in pardoning that we are pardoned;
and it is in dying that we are born to eternal life.
Amen.

RELEASING THE TRIGGER

So, Rachel wondered, you say the prayer and everything's better?

No, the prayer is just the beginning of a process, like learning to swim. You don't go straight from not knowing how to swim, to diving into the deep end of the pool and cutting a mean breaststroke to the other side. First, you get in the water, maybe up to your waist, then you try submerging a bit at a time to see what it's like to be completely underwater and how you can come up for air. You learn to not fear the water and to float. Usually you have someone there with you, talking reassuringly, holding you up at the elbow. You begin to kick your legs and make strokes with your arms to move forward in the water. After several attempts, you're swimming on your own.

Someone belittling for only getting in the water waist high, or floundering on a first attempt to dog paddle, never helped anyone learn. Neither does chastising yourself for not making more progress, moving faster to unearth and defuse your behavior land mines.

Rachel expected herself to do better sooner. "You can intellectually understand a line like 'Grant that I may not so much seek . . . to be loved as to love,'" she said. "But it took praying that for a long time before peace with my past sunk into my heart."

It also took a friend in her support group telling Rachel outright she needed to face the mother who set off all her triggers. "And you have to do better than to face her and forgive her," this friend said. "You have to learn to love her."

Love her? Rachel wondered. *We don't even talk.*

But Rachel wanted release, so she tried. She found her mother home watching television. Rachel had to ask to turn off the TV so they could talk. She had to ask for the conversation. She had to do all the talking, tell her mother, who was unresponsive, how wounding the criticisms had been when she needed encouragement instead. Rachel had to be intentional in keeping the conversation going that day and another and another.

"One day I asked her what her childhood was like," Rachel tells.

"She'd never talked about it. She told me how she was the oldest of five siblings and had to take care of her brothers and sisters. She never had friends of her own. I began to get a glimmer of how she was as wounded as me. I gave her a kiss on the cheek when I left that day."

TRIGGER TALK

Three Ways to Face Your Fears

All these changes to arrest your triggers can overwhelm you. So when the going really gets tough, try three practices for bringing relief that allow you to keep making progress:

- **Deep breathing** helps reduce anxiety, which can trigger both overeating and unhealthy behavior. You can't activate an anxious feeling and your parasympathetic nervous system, which calms you, at the same time. So still yourself and focus on what can restore you. Shut your eyes to avoid distraction and think about your breathing. Pay attention to it. When you're upset, you tend to breathe shallowly and irregularly. You may even, subconsciously, hold your breath like you're going under water. To restore yourself, take a slow, deliberate, deep breath. Think on how the air comes in through your nose and moves down to the very pit of your stomach. Now breathe out through your mouth. For five minutes, alternate taking a regular breath with a deep, slow, down-to-the-pit-of-your-stomach breath. Measure how deeply you're breathing. Put one hand on your abdomen, just below your belly button, and breathe so that you feel your hand rise and fall about an inch each time you exhale. Harvard scientists found (as reported in "Stress Management" in the May 2009 *Harvard Mental Health Letter*) that diaphragmatic breathing, practiced five to twenty minutes, twice a day, for several weeks can heal mind and body.

Rachel's mom was shocked but still unresponsive.

It took many more visits, disclosures, and tender gestures from Rachel before she and her mother had more than a Cold War–type relationship. The day they went to a family gathering, Rachel turned

- **Visualization** helps you accept what's true instead of fearing what's false. In the past you've thought the worst of yourself, and you may struggle now to think any better. But the truth is God says you're wonderfully made (Psalm 139:14) and designed so well that you can do good works (Ephesians 2:10). So fix the eyes of your heart on what's true and noble, excellent and praiseworthy (Philippians 4:8 NIV). Pair deep breathing with some kind of soothing, calming music. Close your eyes to avoid distraction. Think of God by your side, His strong arm holding you, how His hand is so big you can rest in it: bigger than any problem, big enough to part a sea and stop a flood. See yourself strong as God designed you, instead of weak or fat or any other negative thing that would stop you. See yourself as the loving, unafraid person of peace God made you to be. See yourself succeeding in whatever task or path you've set yourself on.
- **Role play** also helps you overcome fear and stay with a situation. The more you do this, the more confidence you gain in knowing you can work through and overcome fear. For instance, maybe there is a person who intimidates you. With a trusted friend or counselor, practice facing this person assertively. Experiment with how to hold your ground and speak your mind with grace. The more you hear yourself able to do so, the more you realize you can actually do so in a real situation. If you're afraid of public speaking, you can role-play on your own at home too. Practice your speech in private, over and over, and you'll increase your confidence in public.

a corner. "It was a transforming moment. Even as we walked through the door, my grandparents were mercilessly criticizing my mother and one another. For the first time, I saw my mom was a wounded person too, not just someone who wounded me."

That's where forgiveness and love began to take root. Rachel's mother never asked for either, and she wouldn't. But love, God tells us, covers a multitude of wrongs (1 Peter 4:8). Rachel could love the one who wounded her and found that doing so gave her the confidence to work on her own unhealthy behaviors. She tried to ask herself before acting:

- Does this matter for a moment or a lifetime?
- How does this action serve others and me in a healthy way?

These two questions can get you closer to living the St. Francis prayer: "For it is in giving that we receive, it is in pardoning that we are pardoned." But it doesn't mean that the hearts of those who wrong you—who planted the land mines that triggered you to eat or act in unhealthy ways—will also be healed.

WRITING YOUR RELEASE

Rachel's mother never did change. She is still critical in mean ways. She still cares more about appearances than the heart. But Rachel has changed. She doesn't look to food for comfort. She's learned to identify what triggers her to eat and act in ways that don't help anyone, especially herself. She's found courage from learning how one prayer, one act of forgiveness, one choice to love one day can lead to another. And she keeps on trying to choose these right things because it keeps her whole, not because she expects it to heal her mother.

A letter helped her see all this.

A letter helped Carol too. Gary wasn't willing to give up the drinking binges, the porn addiction, all the things separating him from his wife and family. Some people are more difficult to forgive than others. Some people and situations have hurt us in unimaginable ways—and they are unreachable or gone, perhaps deceased.

There seems no way to make peace with them and the past, no way to empty ourselves of all the hurt.

But there is a way—a way of writing yourself forward.

One of the best exercises I've found is writing a therapeutic letter. In privacy, in a place where you can collect your thoughts, you dare to deal with the problem that has upset your life for a long time. You can be completely forthright and honest, put everything in writing. You don't need to be a writer. The letter need not be fancy. It can be written by hand on loose-leaf paper or typed at the computer and printed. The form doesn't matter. What you say does. You can get out all the hurt, anger, disappointment, and ugliness you've felt. You can make a declaration in writing to no longer hold things against another person or situation. You can make a commitment to move on toward better health. You can let people off the hook the way you are being let off the hook undeservedly by God. You are not denying your feelings or stuffing them. You are facing the pain, forgiving others and yourself, and letting go.

You can hold this in your hands as long as you need to, look at it, put it down when you feel overwhelmed, and come back to it when you're ready. This is an incredibly empowering and enabling way to deal with the land mines.

"Telling Gary in a letter how hurt I was by him because I really did love him and was mourning our lost way of loving each other was so good. It helped me recuperate in spirit. I realized all my anger at him was because I cared so much. It helped me reclaim a part of my soul, the part I'd tried to cover with food and busyness. I'd moved forward from hard things with my eating, and I could keep moving forward through hard things in my marriage, with a new spirit. Getting all this on paper helped me see it clearly. Putting the paper away was a symbolic act that sort of turned a key in my mind to opening a door of freedom. Even if Gary wasn't changed, I'd declared my change, I'd looked at it and decided I liked what I saw. I didn't want to go down because he chose to—I wanted to be strong and have a hand ready to offer when he might choose to get up."

This was one of the first times I'd heard Carol talk about herself in her family in such a strong, healthy way.

That's what a declaration on paper, a prayer, a choice, a willingness to see can do. It shows you how brave and beautiful you are and can be. You've talked to yourself in the worst ways (*I'm so fat, stupid, not worth others treating me well . . .*). But just as someone criticizing you for not being able to jump in the ocean and swim does not help you cross to another shore, self-abuse in eating or in behaviors like caretaking, and all the mean things you tell yourself, will not help you move forward or live free.

Everyone needs more grace, more forgiveness. Your prayers trigger God to show grace, forgiveness, and love He longs to give—not because we deserve it but because He desires it. He tells us this in a beautiful letter (Jeremiah 29:11–13 NIV): "I know the plans I have for you, . . . plans to prosper you and not to harm you, plans to give you hope and a future. Then you will call on me and come and pray to me, and I will listen to you. You will seek me and find me when you seek me with all your heart."

He shows us how grace will get us through the minefields—both the grace we give and the grace we accept from Him.

You may think the first step is going to kill you. It takes such courage to conquer the behavior that not only triggered you to eat, but triggers you even after you stop bingeing and keeps you spinning in the cycle of actions that only hurt, never heal. But you will find each step, prayer, choice, letter, and letting go helps you get through. No matter if you're shy or bold, a princess or a pauper, reluctant or ready, each step brings you toward the freedom you seek.

ELEVEN

Sweet Surrender

The first day Jack, forty-four, came to recovery group he wasn't so sure he'd find answers, but he had plenty of questions.

"Why can't I beat this thing when I fight every day?" he began.

He had been abusing food for thirty years and was at least sixty pounds overweight. This day he came to us plenty bloodied and bruised too. The night before our session, he'd been in the fight of his life. When I say fight, I mean he was suited up and in the ring. His opponent was famous for a knockdown within seconds.

Jack was no exception.

"I thought I could handle it, really," he said. "I was psyched. I'd talked myself up. I felt good. I'd begun working out." He flexed one arm for good humor, smiling, chuckling at himself—but hurting through it. The fight had been pretty brutal, quick, heartfelt, and no matter how much Jack tried to laugh it away now, he was broken, devastated. He'd gone to an event where there were desserts and chips all around. He thought he could eat just one cookie, just a handful of chips, and get out clean.

He ended up driving from the event straight to a convenience store and loading up on packages of cookies, chips, a few of those greasy hot dogs, and ice cream. He binged liked he hadn't in months, and he felt bloated and ashamed, even though he was laughing, just telling about it.

"Had you ever been able to make it past even one round before, one handful?"

The question from Bethany, sitting to Jack's right, wasn't meant to be unkind.

Jack knew that. Still, he squirmed in his seat. "No." He shrugged. "But I was really ready this time—"

"When you're fighting a food addiction and you're still dancing around with certain foods, you'll never be ready," Julie interrupted. She knew. She'd shared about plenty of her own knockdowns in the not-too-recent past.

"Right," Bethany added. "There's never a 'this time.'" She knew from personal experience too.

You can't win one round with what triggers you. You can't even get in the ring. You're out before you're even in.

The Cookie in Hand Will Always Win

Most of us don't end up looking at our eating problems as addictions until we've been just as beat up and bruised by the insanity of over-eating and food obsession as Jack.

Bethany, thirty-six, understood this only too well. She had tried most of her life to stay in the ring with her triggers of desserts.

"But—pow!" She put a fist in her other palm. "Knocked down and out every time."

"How did you finally beat it?" Jack asked.

"Beat it?" Bethany smiled. "You never beat it." She winked at me. Bethany wasn't a self-proclaimed fighter with food addiction for nothing. She had tried recovery and then would get back in the ring with her trigger foods, thinking she could have just one cookie, just one dessert . . . which, of course, always led to many more and a relapse, eating binge after eating binge. She white-knuckled her way through her first year of recovery.

"Well, what made you finally give up?" Jack tried again, clearly confused.

"You never give up," Bethany explained. "You don't give in. You give over."

By giving over, she explained, you surrender. But surrendering is not resigning. It's not defeat. It's your defense, your offense, and your only real strategy for success. "It's like getting a Buster to fight your battles."

You Call on Your Buster

"Whoa," mocked Jack, ever the jokester, his way of deflecting the self-loathing he felt. "What's a Buster? I want one!"

"You need one," Bethany said.

"Everyone needs one," Julie agreed.

Buster's a prizefighter with a heart. He's like the big, fast, strong, and invincible football star in high school. He's popular, he has lots of friends who are athletes too, and nobody is going to mess with him. He's dating your sister, and he likes you, the school's scrawny nerd. You're slight and socially awkward and getting teased a lot, picked on by all the bullies. But when Buster sees you're being harassed at school, he steps in and makes it clear he'll personally deal with anyone who tries to mess with you.

Even so, one day the bullies tell you if you don't do their homework, they're going to beat you to a pulp.

You know doing other students' homework is wrong . . . but you can't fight against these guys. You may not be brawny, but you've got lots of brains and you know, unless you have a death wish, you'd be foolish to fight this one. You don't stand a chance at their own game, against even one of the bullies, let alone their band of brothers.

So you call on Buster.

You tell the bullies to show up for a fight after school. Then, instead of you stepping up, you send in Buster. The bullies won't need more than one look at your big, towering, powerful friend before you're off the hook. If you go it alone, you're going to get a beating. But sending in Buster gives you relief. No battle. No fight. No fear. No fallout.

"Like I said," Jack quipped, hearing the story, "I want a Buster. How do I get one?"

You Recognize the Enemy

When you're in for a fight, you first recognize there's an enemy. Every soldier does this. It's one of the first things you do to prepare for battle: recognize the enemy and do everything you can to understand him.

You know fighting food abuse is indeed a battle. You have an enemy and there's no denying who it is. You can't just pretend all foods can be eaten in moderation, that you'll win the fight by exercising willpower over all foods. You know you can't pick up a cookie or an ice cream sandwich and think you'll walk away having only one

TRIGGER TALK

When Surrender's Real, You Can Recoil as from a Hot Flame

Sherry, thirty-eight, fought hard for recovery over more than a year. Every day was a battle to stay the course. All the while, she worried about not losing weight fast enough, not managing well enough the issues that drove her to eat. She berated herself over this.

"Then one evening I realized I'd done all I could do that day. I did my best. For a change, instead of railing at God for why I wasn't better, why everything was so hard, I thanked Him for helping me." That night, the first in a long time, Sherry went to sleep completely at peace because she knew there was nothing more she could have done that day and any good result would be by God's grace.

The next day, doing all the right things didn't seem so much a battle as "just what I do," she said. The day after became easier, and the day after that too. What seemed a war became a way of life.

"You don't believe it in the beginning, but following what

sweet taste and no other damage. That's as foolish as the boy who carried around a rattlesnake.

The boy's story is told in dozens of variations by different cultures throughout the world.[1] He's walking down a path and comes upon a rattlesnake. The boy stops but the snake coaxes him closer.

"Please," the rattler begs. "Can you take me to the top of the mountain? I'm old and hope to see the sunset one last time before I die."

"No!" the boy says, backing away. "If I pick you up, you will bite me and I will surely die."

you know to work and surrendering to it, not fighting it, brings you to a place of living free," Sherry said. "Doing the right things becomes natural. So does turning from your triggers."

In the *Alcoholics Anonymous Big Book*, this is what is often referred to as recoiling as from a hot flame. You no longer have to consciously tell yourself, "Danger! There's danger ahead," when you're in a situation or facing a food that will trigger you to abuse food. You simply draw away instantly, instinctively, naturally, as from a red-hot burner. If you didn't, you know you'd get burned. You've learned, like the toddler, living free of the pain is just better than giving in to the curiosity of what it's like to touch what's dangerous.

Sherry knew recoiling as from the hot flame had become true for her the day friends dropped by with a surprise gift: a blackberry pie made from the spoils of a mountain outing.

"They didn't know I'd abused food and, for once, it didn't seem questionable or agonizing to explain it to them. I simply made it clear I couldn't and wouldn't eat the dessert, and I thanked them for their kindness. My reaction wasn't an ordeal for once. It was automatic."

"Oh, pleassse," the snake begs again. "I promissse I won't bite you. Pleassse take me up to the mountain."

The boy shifts and slowly moves round the snake. *The sunset would be beautiful to see from the top of the mountain.* "Okay," he says, and picks up the snake, holding it close to his chest. He begins walking with the snake held tightly, safely, and climbs to the top of the mountain. He sets the snake down and together they watch the sinking sun, so beautiful with its colors and slow-motion dance, until it is dark.

"Oh, thank you," the snake whispers. "Can you take me home now? I'm tired."

Though full of wonder from their time together, the boy is tired too. So he picks up the snake, holds him close to his chest, tightly, safely, and treks back down the mountain. They've shared such an amazing day together the boy brings the snake home, gives him a warm place to sleep, feeds him. They become friends. They live like that for a while.

One day, the snake pleads, "Can you take me to my home now? It's time for me to leave this world."

"Of course," the boy says. He's sad to see his friend go; they've shared some good times together. But the boy is willing to do whatever his friend asks because he has come under the snake's spell. Carefully the boy picks up the rattler, holds it close, tightly, safely to his chest and makes his way back to the road where they met.

As the boy sets the rattler down gently, tenderly, sad to see his friend go, the snake turns and bites him in the chest.

The boy cries in pain. "Why did you do that? Now I shall surely die!"

The snake is already slipping into the grass. "But, my boy," he says, slithering away, "you always knew what I was when you picked me up."

You know what triggers you before you even pick them up. You know trigger foods are no friend and as much an enemy as a poisonous snake. You can carry around a cake. You can keep the pudding in the fridge and doughnuts in a drawer, and maybe you can live to-gether awhile. But eventually you're going to get bit, you're going to get hurt, you're going to kill yourself keeping the enemy within reach.

It's not just the food that's your enemy either. It's the mind-set of dieting and obsession to lose weight and get fit that can be disguised as your friends too.

"I spent hundreds, probably thousands of dollars on diet plans, exercise equipment, gym memberships," Bethany told Jack in sup-port group. "These things weren't exactly an enemy. They weren't bad investments. They just weren't the whole answer. They actually became props I used to bully myself into thinking I could beat my enemy, the addiction, the abusive behavior, by spending more time with them, working them harder as my answer, my solution."

The props are no Buster. They won't fight for you. You can use the props for the fight, but they can be part of enemy forces if you let them.

When you know the trigger foods will trip you, like an enemy that goes in for the kill and takes no prisoners, and the addictive and abusive behavior will work against you, then you know you can't get into a fight with them. You'll lose. You need to surrender to the fact and stop handling what has such a powerful grip on you.

Does this mean put down the workout weights, don't touch a food plan, give up on fitness programs?

No. It means call in your Buster to help you walk away from what will strike you down, the trigger foods and the "I can do it on my own" mentality. So when your support group, counseling work, and food plan aren't keeping you from a tempting dessert or trigger food and a binge, you can call on God, your Buster, who will always steer you clear of the snakes.

You Go Another Way

When it comes to sugar and other foods that trigger food abuse, you have to follow what you know will keep you from the madness. It means you don't climb into the ring with what you know will bring you down.

You can't say you'll eat just one slice of pie when you've got a history of never stopping after one slice. You can't say you'll have just a handful or two of potato chips when you've never eaten less than the whole bag at a time. You can't pretend you're going to win against those prizefighting trigger foods because the cookie will always win. The chips will never lose.

You don't climb into the ring with what you know will bring you down.

So you fight another way. You choose another way. You go a different course, the one of surrender by calling on your Buster and freeing yourself from what otherwise is a sure knockdown and knockout, a beating by the desserts and the fast food. You may think this signifies a weakness, but it really means sanity. Would you put yourself in the path of the speeding truck? Would you suit up to go even one round with Muhammad Ali at the height of his career?[2]

There's a wonderful poem that illustrates this process of confronting the prizefighter foods and surrendering to a power greater than your own by not even getting into the ring. "Autobiography in Five Short Chapters"[3] shows what it looks like to call upon your Buster as another way of fighting:

I.

I walk down the street.
There is a deep hole in the sidewalk.
I fall in.
I am lost . . . I am helpless.
It isn't my fault.
It takes me forever to find a way out.

II.

I walk down the same street.
There is a deep hole in the sidewalk.
I pretend I don't see it.

I fall in again.
I can't believe I am in the same place.
But, it isn't my fault.
It still takes a long time to get out.

III.

I walk down the same street.
There is a deep hole in the sidewalk.
I see it is there.
I still fall in . . . it's a habit.
my eyes are open
I know where I am.
It is my fault.
I get out immediately.

IV.

I walk down the same street.
There is a deep hole in the sidewalk.
I walk around it.

V.

I walk down another street.

At the start of choosing recovery from food addiction, you think you can take on anything. You think your will can get you through, but you fail. You just don't see that trigger foods will swallow you when you take even a taste of them. Then you flounder in their grip. You can deny and pretend away the power of the trigger foods for a long time. Even when you begin to realize the triggers will always bring you down, you still can fall under their power because you haven't yet changed your course and you dance in the ring with them, and the dance, the fight, has become a habit. You can go down this road a long time before you realize you've got to go another way.

Choosing to go a different way is not an act of cowardice, not chickening out. It's an act of sanity. It's smart. It's powerful. It's an act that says you're not giving up or in, but you are giving over the craziness of going down the same road and expecting to arrive at a different place. You're optioning to call in Buster and change not only your course, but the course of changes for you—you're not trying to make it happen on your own. It is exhausting and will leave you as broken and devastated as Jack found himself when he finally reached out for support. When you choose to go another way, you choose to let Buster fight for you and stick to the most powerful thing you can do, which is, ironically, all you ever could do anyway.

TWELVE

Do What You Can
and Let God Do the Rest

So now you have a Buster—be it your support group, a plan, whoever and whatever. You understand God is ready to fight for you, and you know what He can do for you, what He longs to do for you. But what does that mean? That you just pray to Him for help, call on Him, and everything immediately gets better?

God can do anything. He makes miracles every day. Who knows exactly how God does what He does? It is a mystery.[1] Yet while we don't know the ins and outs of His ways, His will is clear: He means for us to do what we can, and surrender everything else, especially the change and transformation itself, to His power, not our own. We know, after all, from all the knockdowns, all the walks down Trigger Road, our own power is limited.

A great example of this for me came as a young woman in the arena of public speaking. Because of the shame, insecurities, and self-loathing I felt growing up due to food and weight issues, I never wanted to call attention to myself. Standing in front of even a few people for any length of time was the last thing I ever thought I could do.

So when I began working on recovery from food abuse, I attended support group meetings, and it turned out everyone was asked to share their stories and experiences. I was terrified. But others believed in me, encouraged me, and cheered me on—and I did it. Speaking to the group became easier as we got to know one another.

Then I was asked to be a keynote speaker at a weekend conference, where a couple hundred people would be in attendance. *There is no way I can do this*, I thought; all the old fears seized me, threatening to stop me.

> God means for us to do what we can, and surrender everything else, especially the change and transformation itself, to His power, not our own.

Still colleagues and friends said, "You can." "You will be great." "You have so much to say." "Do it!"

I *did* have a lot to say, things I wanted to share to help others, so I agreed. But the morning I was scheduled to give my first of a series of talks, I began to panic. *What made me possibly think I could do this? I can't do this!* I wanted to run away. I made my way to a chapel near where I was to appear to try and focus and collect myself. For thirty minutes or more, I prayed. I told God honestly how unprepared I felt, how incapable and afraid.

Over those thirty minutes, I felt an increasing rush of peace instead of panic, and sense of calling instead of incapability.

I walked back to where I was to speak—and I did stand in front of the crowd and speak with power and enthusiasm. I had done all I could do, and surrendered all the rest to God. He worked out something good in me and others.

Sound mystical? Miraculous? Mind-boggling?

Yes, yes, yes, for me. This is also a picture of how surrender is so very practical and real. There are things you do—all that you can—and then surrendering the rest to God allows Him to do the miracle, the mind-boggling, magnificent things you can't.

Look at the practical, tangible things I did:

- **Agreed to step up to what was asked of me.** I said yes, even to something out of my comfort zone.
- **Opened up myself to receive support.** I engaged with the encouragement given, took on the faith others put in me, and let their faith carry me until I could move forward in my own faith in myself.

- **Stayed in conversation with God**, telling Him my fears and listening for His comfort, receiving the courage He offered: "Do not be afraid, for I am with you" (Genesis 26:24, Isaiah 43:5 NIV).
- **Asked God** to work beyond my own power.
- **Trusted Him** to use me and the situation for His will. I had prayed, "Let Your words fill my mouth," and He honored that. I speak frequently in my work, and even now I get a little nervous before stepping in front of a crowd, but when I do what I can do and surrender the rest to God, He makes a miracle out of what would otherwise be a mess.

Agreeing, stepping up, opening yourself to receive support, engaging, praying to God and listening for His comfort, and then recognizing His trust is not in vain: these things don't sound like the ways to fight. It's so counterintuitive that these actions can defeat an enemy. Yet when God is involved, when you surrender to your own limitations and call, wait, ask, watch, recognize, and give Him power, the battle is over before it's begun.

God can do what we cannot.

For those of us who are intelligent and analytical, surrendering to this truth is difficult, even when we love God and believe He will do what He says He will do. What we need to focus on, though, is it might not be right away. We may have to call on Him again and again and again—for one hour, and then work at it again for one hour more, and one more. Rather than get bogged down in this, though, we must focus on the bigger picture: God is in the ring and He'll go as many rounds as needed to keep us safe and moving forward.

One Day at a Time

This is one of the most important principles of surrender. You don't just do it once and are then done with it. Surrender is not an act of giving up or resignation, but of giving over, a process. It makes surrender one of the most difficult things in addiction to grasp. No matter if you don't have to go in the ring. No matter if you know recovery takes a whole package of things, not just a pill to pop and make you better, or a plan to follow and expect your behavior to change too. You'll be no exception to grappling with surrender. There's something in our psyche, no matter how much faith we have in God, or how much fortitude in handling tough things, that can always rise and say, "*I* can do this. *I* will do this."

When I talk to people about giving up sugar, they usually react in horror or defeat. "How can I possibly stop cold turkey?" is a typical response. "I've never gone a week, let alone a whole month, without something sweet!"

When I talk about giving transformation some time, taking off the pressure of seeing the weight drop tomorrow, there's usually protest. "You mean you don't think I should try to see some physical results this month? But don't I have to see some weight loss, once I cut out all the food triggers?!"

When I suggest that making peace with the past is going to take hard work over the next few months, maybe years, depending on the issues, there usually are groans. "Why would I bother signing up for all this work if I can't expect change and relief soon? Not a lot of incentive there to do this, is there?"

Isn't there? Your next hour can be free of anxiety and the craziness of abuse and addiction, and the hour after that can be better, and tomorrow can be even better, and next week can be the best yet. Your miracle is one step or stage away. Who's to say the thing you do next or the one after that isn't when God will restore a good, clean, healthy life to you?

You can't predict if there will be bullies who come your way next month, but you can lean on God right now. You can do the next thing for the next hour. You can follow your food plan for breakfast and then lunch and then dinner. You can go to the next support group meeting, and then the next. You can take a walk around this corner as part of your stress-relief and workout plan—and, who knows, maybe you can go around two corners tomorrow, and a mile the next day.

Progress comes one step at a time, and your healing and recovery take place with each healthy choice.

Of course, the difficulty is in the waiting. What's one to do when waiting anyway?

Surrender the Need to Rush

Living in a microwave, fast-food, ATM generation, we want everything now, instantly, on demand—or sooner, please.

I was no exception when I began my recovery. I wanted to see results—namely, weight loss—immediately. I couldn't wait, and so I kept trying harder, I kept doing more exercise, I went to more meetings, I . . . see what I mean?

I, I, I. I was trying to do everything on my own. *I* hadn't surrendered at all. *I* was stuck in the "I" mentality.

The results of the "I" mentality are just what you'd expect. If you haven't heard this truth already, you are sure to hear it in recovery: when you place one foot in yesterday and one foot in tomorrow, you will fall down today.

You can't straddle yesterday and tomorrow. You can only do what you can now. Trying to do otherwise leaves you in a place vulnerable to getting stuck or stopped. Yesterday is

> **When you place one foot in yesterday and one foot in tomorrow, you will fall down today.**

filled with the shame of your food abuse and tomorrow is filled with the anxiousness of what the bullies said they would do to you. Today is where you can do the next thing. Today is where you can take care of what's needed now, whether it is eating a good meal and avoiding a trigger food, or charging up on God with a prayer or some of His promises, or dealing with the anger and frustration that used to drive you to eat.

Surrender the Need to Sacrifice

Most of us who are food addicts don't have a clue about how to take care of ourselves. For too long we've tried to care for ourselves with food. We've fed our frustrations with Twinkies, our anger with pasta. We've stuffed our emotions along with tubs of whipped cream and cans of frosting. Because the food hasn't ultimately fed

TRIGGER TALK

When You Worship the Fridge and Food

God will fight for you to beat your eating issues, but are you ready to take a stand and fight where you can?

What about right before the fridge? Think about it. How many times have you come home from a stressful day or dealt with the kids or a boss who won't listen, and in frustration gone to the refrigerator? You didn't kneel down or pray as at a religious altar, but you looked inside and you grabbed something to eat. Maybe you toyed with the idea of that a long time before getting there; you orbited around that moment just like an idol worshipper before the golden calf.

Meanwhile, God is fighting hard for you and is so jealous of the fridge and the food you've put before Him (Exodus 20:4–5 and Deuteronomy 6:15).

What? You think you haven't worshipped the fridge and food? Any time you dwell on something and center your life on it, you're in danger of making it an idol. Now, as you've begun to fight for food to be in its rightful place, you may have made new things your idols: an obsession with having the perfect body, losing weight, thinking all day about what to eat or how many calories and fat grams or carbohydrates are in a particular food. You can stop the all-day affair with—and worship of—food, weight, calories, and exercise by

- **changing the channel in your head** from thinking of food to meditating upon God's power, goodness, and help. When your thoughts spiral onto matters of food, deliberately focus

our emotional needs, and we're ashamed, we've tended to those around—children, spouse, coworkers, the job itself, friends—before ourselves, as a form of penance or atonement. We've fought the

instead on God's grace. Let His promises drown out your worries. Keep at hand God's promises that nothing is too difficult for Him (Jeremiah 32:17) and that He is gracious, merciful, and great in lovingkindness (Psalm 145:8). Write these on an index card to tuck in a pocket or tape to a kitchen cupboard. You can also type in and save these promises as a text message you can reread in an instant on your cell phone.

- **proclaiming your trust in God.** Make Psalm 20:7 your own: "Some boast in chariots and some in horses, but we will boast in the name of the LORD." Substitute words like *diets* and *workouts* for *chariots* and *horses,* and *I* for *we.* God loves to be called upon to help you, and He doesn't always show up when or how we might expect. But He promises to always work things for our good (Romans 8:28–39): "We overwhelmingly conquer through Him who love[s] us."
- **throwing away your scale.** It's too easy to make your happiness dependent every day (and sometimes three times a day) by the numbers on the scale. If you want to know if you're losing weight, check on a scale once a month. The point is if you can't stop obsessing over it, get rid of the scale. When you're eating right you don't need to be checking.
- **lightening up and stopping the legalism.** Instead of thinking you need to always prayerfully consider every morsel of food you eat, stick to your plan as best you can. Now let go and watch what He will do, giving Him the glory for all good results because you've already acknowledged His power. This means you can be free to receive His work, knowing He will do something good in you, for you, and through you.

stereotypes that overweight people (and most of us are overweight, obese even, as a result of the binges) are lazy, careless, and indulgent.[2] And the way we've fought is with one more binge after another.

You know the result. For all the self-sacrifice, self-flagellation, and self-destruction, you're left broken and devastated like Jack. You may try to deflect the pain of this, but the truth is you've carried the snake too long. You've gone too many rounds with the prizefighter who dances like a butterfly, then stings like a bee.[3]

When you begin recovery, when you choose to surrender, you put down the snake. You get out of the ring. You get your chance to take care of yourself for a change. You decide not to get beat up or go through life broken and devastated.

You call on God. You ask Him to fight your battles while you do the only things you can—the next things—for yourself. So while God goes to work, you stick to your food plan. You eat your three meals a day and the two planned snacks too, so you don't feel deprived. You share your frustrations and fears in a support group and receive encouragement and practical ideas for how to go forward— what thing to do next. You call on God and fill up on His promises and love for you. You power up and put down a new root that feeds your surrender—and your success. You become tethered and strengthened by that root, the root called *trust*.

Surrender the Need to Know

Trust can be as difficult to understand as surrender because they are sisters. You cannot have one without the other. But trying to explain how it works is like trying to explain to the student driver there will come a day when you don't think about all the things you have to do to move forward—you'll just get in the car, buckle up, and go.

When you're first learning to drive, just getting in the car and going forward can seem daunting. You have to think through every little thing to watch and do so you can pass the driving test and get your license, your freedom.

All the things you have to know and do can definitely be a little scary. Certainly, there's some danger of getting out of control. You practice driving and read up on the laws for motorists. There's so much you feel responsible to know.

Your goal is freedom to be able to just hop in the car and go, get where you need to anytime, anywhere. So you go to take the test for your license and you're careful to watch your speed, stay in your lane at all times, keep the vehicle in line (especially when parallel parking!), and watch for speed bumps and potholes. You check your mirrors and look over your shoulder to change lanes, watch the lights and the signs, look all directions before turning. You're trying hard to think on all these things and be perfect with every function. You're trying to anticipate and know about everything that's ahead so you can get to your goal to become a licensed driver and drive freely.

Of course, you can't know everything that's ahead, predict all you'll encounter. Yet, in time, doing the right things to get you safely where you're going becomes rote. You don't even think about them, and you don't have to worry about knowing everything you'll encounter along the way because all your experience develops your instincts, reactions, and choices. You eventually just get in the car and . . . drive.

So it is with beating addiction by trusting God to fight for you. You don't know everything that's ahead, but you know He will fight for you. There's no way to understand the ins and outs of His ways, but you know His will is for you to call on Him and to do the next thing.

Lean not on your own understanding, God says (Proverbs 3:5–6). He'll make the way straight for you. He'll go before you as you drive toward recovery and success. Lean on Him and not your own understanding. This is what it means to trust: go, drive, do to the very best of your ability each stretch of road, one trip at a time—and He will get you there. He will take away your compulsion to eat. He will make you sane regarding food. He will give you peace in your relationship with food. He will help your body strengthen.

He will fight for you.

PART THREE

Beating Your Triggers: A Plan

I can do all things through Him who strengthens me.

—PHILIPPIANS 4:13

THIRTEEN

Trigger-Free Eating

When Karen, a thirty-six-year-old new mom, came to my office she was at least seventy pounds overweight and miserable. She admitted during pregnancy she gained a lot more than baby weight, using it as a reason to indulge in even more snacks and desserts than normal. She'd hit 225 pounds, her highest on the scales (she's just five feet five inches tall). But it wasn't the pounds she gained while carrying the baby that troubled her most. It was the exhaustion and defeat, the shame she felt from episodes of overeating.

Since age thirteen, when Karen ate a whole carton of ice cream after a boyfriend break-up, she had turned to food for comfort. Whenever she felt anxious, rejected, happy, sad, stressed—pretty much any high or low occasion—she reached for potato chips and ice cream instead of a phone or a friend to deal with her emotions.

Then the nurse placed her newborn baby girl in her arms. Karen instantly fell in love with little Madeline. She wanted to give Maddy the world, the moon, not an overweight mom troubled by food issues. To do that and set a healthy example, Karen knew she needed to finally address what she admitted was becoming debilitating.

It took her eight months to make it to my office. She'd tried one more diet, achieved some results, then binged again. A few binges more and she gained back every bit of what she'd lost.

"I'll do whatever it takes to be healthy, make my daughter as proud of me as I am of her," she said, dropping into a chair. She was motivated, determined. "I want to be able to run with Maddy at the park without having to stop because I'm out of breath." She shook her head. "As it is now, I run out of stamina just carrying her up one flight of stairs."

I smiled. Karen wanted good things for good reasons: freedom from overeating, longevity, to live healthy for herself and the ones she loved.

Every day I talk with clients who pledge the same thing. Some have more serious issues, actually hoarding food to binge through the day. Others deal with being triggered to overeat now and then. Regardless, both kinds of clients usually get to this dreaded question pretty quickly in a consultation.

Karen didn't waste another minute getting right to what she really came for—the question and focus that always makes my heart sink: "So what's the diet that will work best for me?"

THE TRUTH ABOUT DIETS

Like Karen, maybe you've come to solve overeating issues with a diet or an eating plan alone. I know it may be the very reason some of you bought this book, and maybe you turned straight to this chapter wanting a dos and don'ts food list.

This is the essence of why so many of us finally face our eating issues. We're desperate to know: What can I eat? What diet will get me started on my way to the perfect body? We're tired of carrying so much extra weight on our bones—and in our hearts, minds, and souls. We want to be lighter, look better, experience true freedom.

What ultimately transforms us is not the diet alone but how we think and feel about food, our relationship with it and others. And what (and sometimes who) drives us to eat, and how much, and when, and why. No diet alone can resolve it all. This is why the diet is never *the* answer, and a food plan is *part* of the answer. Transformation happens from the inside out, and shows up not just in the body but in the mind and in the soul. *Whatever it takes to lose weight* is not the goal. *Whatever it takes to live healthy and restore a right relationship in mind, body, and spirit* is.

That's so important before we even talk about food plans because if you avoid true transformation and skip the other chapters in this book just to try the trigger-free eating ideas, you'll end up like Karen. You'll be right back where you started, only feeling worse for trying and not finding success. Addressing food issues with a diet alone is like trying to use a power saw without the power. A diet just won't cut it. Restricting food alone won't get you very far. You've got to fuel your mind and spirit as well as your body.

> **Addressing food issues with a diet alone is like trying to use a power saw without the power.**

Karen learned this the hard way. She left my office after our first meeting, nodding in agreement that she wanted true transformation. In the weeks that followed, we began to look at and work on the things that would trigger her to eat a whole carton of cookies in one sitting or snack the entire day. But once Karen got the food plan, I didn't see her.

She returned to my office nearly a year later, fifty pounds lighter but starting to regain the weight. She dropped into the office chair with a new kind of defeat.

"There's no hope for me on this diet," she said. She really had been motivated too. Determined. She had stuck to the food plan . . . except for the times cravings got the best of her; the returning episodes of eating an entire bag of kettle chips with a whole container of dip, because she was lonely when her husband was away on business; the swings by Burger King for a couple of bacon double cheeseburgers, because she was frustrated with Maddy's fussiness on a grocery shopping trip.

There is little hope, I agreed, in trying to solve food issues with diet alone.

Why Diets Won't Work

It's true most everyone, at some point in life, looks for ways to solve a weight problem. So most people can try the latest diet on the market and find some success with temporary weight loss. They may start out deciding to live completely without carbohydrates or fat. Then, because that's hard, they stray a bit. They take back a little bit of bread, maybe add some butter to the vegetables, a drop of cream to the coffee. That's all it takes to be off to the races again, running with whatever tastes good.

Without ever intending to gain back the weight, that's exactly what they do. But, no problem for those other folks—they can just go back on the diet. They can drop pounds and clothes sizes for a wedding or the summer just because they choose to do so. They can manage to keep off the weight, or, if they do gain it back, start dieting again and get results. There are plenty of people on the earth like this, and they have the capacity to pull in the reins on whatever they eat, and cut back whenever they choose.

But when you're hardwired to be triggered by certain foods, the diet process isn't going to work for you—you can't just lose weight, gain it back, go back on a diet, and expect to have a good hold on the reins of what's been a runaway pattern of eating all your life. In fact, you can't rely on a diet at all.

The diet was never the real issue in the first place.

Take a look at what Karen did before she even came to me. She began one of the best diets around, WeightWatchers, a program with a healthy and balanced food plan that's completely livable. People on WeightWatchers take off weight all the time in a balanced and healthy manner . . . unless, that is, they are people hardwired with a food trigger.

Foods Still Trigger

The problem of diets for the overeater is there are things like exchanges, and desserts with sugar and white flour. People not hardwired to overeat will be very happy for a nice, measured dessert. Telling someone like Karen she can have one WeightWatchers dessert is like putting a bowl of ice cream in front of a child and saying, "All right, you can have one spoonful for the day and that's it."

One spoonful just isn't going to happen. Neither is just one very lovely, measured dessert. When you're hardwired to overeat, you'll never feel satisfied. One taste of what triggers your craving will start the cycle of overeating all over again. So, even when you intend to follow the plan, it's likely the whole box of WeightWatchers desserts will be gone before day's end.

> **One taste of what triggers your craving will start the cycle of overeating all over again.**

Exchanges Give Too Much Flexibility

The exchanges in diet plans represent a similar problem. The idea behind exchanges is to give you some slack, a margin for those occasions when you can't weigh and measure, or know exactly what you're going to eat. So the food plan allows you so much carbohydrate and fat foods per day, and if you eat them at lunch, then you just exchange what's on the plan for dinner and omit the things eaten already.

Sound reasonable?

Not for someone like Karen or me or you. That margin is disastrous, a margin for error, in fact. Exchanges give too much flexibility for people like us with a track record of not thinking well on our feet about food choices. We can go out to a business lunch at a restaurant and decide, since we're going to enjoy the good food prepared for us, we'll exchange the carbohydrates and fats we'd normally have for dinner for what we'll enjoy right here, right now, and skip them at dinner.

By dinnertime, though, we still want our carbs and fats. So we go ahead and eat them and feel guilty for breaking with the food plan, the one where we've been learning to weigh and measure, but have not yet grasped the measurement of a little and a lot. We think because we've messed up a little, we may as well go ahead and mess up a lot. So we have the carb and fat for dinner, in addition to what we ate at lunch. We also decide since we'll start over tomorrow, we may as well really blow it tonight.

See how it works?

Tomorrow is a big deal. *Tonight* and *right now* are what we're used to dealing with, and that leads to another of the root reasons diets don't work for us.

Deprivation Can Undo You

Dieting often leaves people feeling hungry and deprived. Either there isn't enough satisfying food or there are missing, needed food groups, and the restrictions become too difficult to stick with long term. (To be clear, cutting out sugar and refined carbohydrates because they trigger you to overeat isn't dieting any more than it is to abstain from eating strawberries because you're deathly allergic to them. When we're talking about dieting here, we're talking about the whole psychology to restrain yourself from foods to lose weight, not abstain to stay well.)

As Karen learned, trying a diet alone, she often felt deprived by consuming the exchanges at one meal and not being allowed to have them at the next. The deprivation felt more like punishment to her, and she already felt punished enough in other areas, which was what drove her to binge and overeat (and why the food plan alone is never the way to freedom). So she wasn't going to let dinner beat her down too.

She began to compensate the only way she knew how. She fed her food cravings and overate. Then she tried depriving herself again. And again. And again. And the cycle continued.

Quick Loss Leads to a Fast Fail

The same thing happens with quick weight loss plans, which often eliminate major food groups for a period of time. We buy into them because we've been so ashamed of our eating issues and weight, we're desperate to see change. Too many of us think: *I just need a jump start. I'll take off some weight for the wedding, then I'll switch to a less-restrictive diet. I can't stand living fat another day, so I'm going to juice fast to feel better now.*

But we can't keep to such restrictions. We break from them. The cycle of sneaking and hiding no-no foods, of starving and bingeing, then slipping into the pattern of overeating, continues. This creates even more shame, the sense of even greater failure and defeat. The sad, damaging, and paradoxical thing is that in the end often more weight is gained back than was lost, and now the body has gotten out of whack. Recovery can become even more difficult.

Counting Calories Becomes Obsession

Dieters learn to count their fats and carbohydrates, calories and grams, and they're okay. But too often overeaters get lost in this. If we've read a lot of diet books, we're already completely confused about food. What one book says is healthful, another calls bad. We don't know what to believe anymore, so we start out trying to manage the numbers and choices. We worry about too much of this or too much of that. Every gram becomes a gigantic issue we try to justify. Calorie counting becomes one more obsession. Management turns to manipulation.

The truth is it's not the calories or fats in our moderate meals that cause the problem with our weight. It's the bingeing and sneaking between planned meals. We get caught up in worrying about eating the high-fat salad dressing at lunch, then two hours later down a dozen doughnuts and a bag of Doritos.

If this is where you've found yourself trapped, don't despair. The years of dieting experience will be useful when you're ready to beat triggers and conquer overeating and food addiction. By dieting, you've learned a bit about portions and nutritional facts. That's good. Now consider when we go ahead and eat the salad dressing and the rest of the healthy foods we need, our bodies process the food better and we feel fuller. We're less likely to binge. It works out. So we need to give up the diet mentality and stop obsessing about the details of every morsel of healthy food we eat. In fact, changing your thinking is going to be as important as a food plan.

Changing Patterns Versus Losing Weight

Marianne learned this. Like Karen, Marianne discovered the food plan begins with a mind plan, a spirit plan. She started out thinking she just needed a guide on what to eat and not eat. By age forty-one, she had tried all the strict programs. On one, she rigidly weighed and measured foods. On another, she completely abstained from carbohydrates. Neither stopped her from eventually downing a whole batch of brownies.

She needed a food plan not focused so much on the foods as on the structure, stability, and constancy, and the identifiable patterns of eating. She needed to focus less on weight loss itself and more on the primary goal of trigger-free eating and bringing sanity to the relationship with food.

First, she needed to accept the idea she didn't just have a weight problem but her brain was hardwired to overeat. Packs of sugar-free gum, constant drinks of Diet Coke, and an occasional sugar-free frozen yogurt became her clue.

You might be shocked. How can those items possibly be a problem?

"The sugar-free frozen yogurt was too close to the real thing for me to handle," Marianne said. The taste of sweet, not just its properties, was a trigger that started her binges again. The same thing happened with the sugar-free gum and Diet Coke. "It was a disgusting, addictive behavior. I would chew one piece of gum until the flavor was gone, then chew another and more, until a pack was finished. Of course, popping a new piece was done in secret just like most of my previous bingeing. The same thing happened with abusing Diet Coke. I'd drink one can after another all day long but pretend I was nursing the same one."

Marianne went through this cycle for years until she found a food plan to keep her from her triggers. "Sugar-free gum and Diet Coke may seem better than bingeing on half gallons of rocky road ice cream," she says, "but it still was insanity. I was slipping and sliding with food during the first two years. How does the saying go? 'You go from a sliver to a slice to a slab to a slob'? I was on that constant slope. I would get it together for a month, two months, then go off my plan, then go on again. I'd be off, on, off, on, until the bingeing and my weight were outrageous."

What worked for others didn't work for her: not the rigid, weighed-and-measured food plans with no carbohydrates; not simply

TRIGGER TALK

What Are Your Food Triggers?

You may already know in your heart what sets you off on a binge or overeating. For instance, if you eat something to calm the inner turmoil you feel, and it then becomes the reason for turmoil, it's a trigger. Maybe one slice of cheesecake turns into downing the whole thing. Maybe allowing yourself one hand-ful of chips leads you to empty the new bag. Maybe volume is your trigger, and you get the supersized lunch special at the drive-through, then your supersized cravings lead to ordering more.

It's helpful to call out your triggers, specifically and offi-cially. Look at them, just as an emergency room doctor reads about all the symptoms before going to work. On a sheet of paper, in writing, reflect upon and respond to the following:

- When I see or taste this food, I need more.
- I think about this food (how often, how much?).
- This food makes me happy.
- I was so upset I went (where) and ate (what).
- I went out (alone or with whom?) to celebrate over this food.
- When I'm alone (and feeling how?) I eat this food (how much and how often?).

sticking to three meals a day with nothing in between, or three meals with one planned snack or two planned snacks, or snacking on dried fruit. "The problem wasn't in what I tried, but in the fact that I needed to watch the trigger foods I put in my mouth, and why, and there's no question all of this acting out was keeping me overeating."

For instance, the sweet taste was a trigger, so eating even a piece of dried fruit turned into downing the whole bag. So was volume. "I tried to get away with eating three-bean salad on the salad bar," Marianne explained, "until my salads were big enough to feed two or three people."

To change, she needed to address the eating behavior. A first step was knowing what triggered her.

Most common triggers are foods with sugar (typically the most addictive ingredient for food addicts), white flour, or refined carbohydrates. Maybe you have to avoid all three of these ingredients equally. Everyone's different. Some recovering food addicts can eat no starchy foods at all. Others can still eat grains like brown rice and potatoes, but never any flour products. Some folks can eat whole-grain breads and pastas, maybe even white flour to varying degrees. For some people their trigger isn't so much a specific food as the volume they consume—one big meal or snack gets them going into a binge. For others, salty and fatty foods are the triggers. The severity of the problem and levels of what can be tolerated without triggering a binge differ.

But it's good to know that, in more severe cases, food addictions are like substance abuse. Where one addict finds pleasure in taking sedatives, another prefers stimulants. Some like to drink. Others prefer to smoke. Some do it alone. Others prefer company. Some hide what they're doing. Some don't care what anyone thinks—and don't realize how out of control they really are.

As you begin to follow an eating plan, don't expect each new step to be the total answer. Expect some trial and error. Expect that what worked for someone else needs adaptations for you.

So the big question: What can you eat?

Start by keeping a food diary this week. Get a cheap notebook, nothing so fancy or expensive you're too self-conscious to just scribble down notes in it. By day, and throughout each day, write down everything you eat, when (the time can be illuminating), and why (what you were feeling before, during, and after). Be sure to include the amount of food you eat, as close as you can figure. If you ate a carton of cupcakes, how many were in there? For now, just clip the ingredient label from the carton and tape it into your diary.

Realistically, you might loathe documenting what you've tried to hide for years, so this exercise may be difficult, alarming even. Do it anyway. Remind yourself: *this is a big step forward and this notebook and all it contains will soon be history.*

FOURTEEN

Developing a Food Plan

Most food addiction treatment programs start out with a sugar- and flour-free plan, where you weigh and measure foods at three meals with one or two snacks a day. This is so important because you may have a fairly distorted view of what is a normal portion. While some people can eat cleanly without weighing and measuring, you may need to stick with the scales and measuring cups at the start. You also can expect a typical plan to:

- **be clear and structured.** There need to be boundaries with food, a beginning and end to eating meals. You need to know which foods are good choices and which will trigger you. You'll want something clear enough to keep you from overeating, but loose enough to live in a world where you share meals with others without being tied to one thing. You'll want to commit to three meals a day and maybe one or two planned snacks, preferably around the same times each day.
- **include all the main food groups** and that means complex carbohydrates such as fruits, vegetables, whole grains, lean proteins (fish, poultry, meat, tofu), fats, and dairy. You'll want the foods necessary for health.
- **satisfy hunger.** It's important to have a plan that satisfies and doesn't leave you feeling hungry. The guiding principle is there needs to be enough to eat and not too much. You want a food plan you can live with for the rest of your life, meaning it can't be a restrictive weight-loss plan. Ironically, when you eat well, you get to a weight that's right.

Though there's not one way to eat trigger-free, an example of a weighed-and-measured plan might look like this (and I cannot stress enough that there can be great variations of this, depending on your size, preferences, activity, and triggers, so you will want a nutritionist's guidance in working out something more precise and tailored for you):

Breakfast: 1 ounce protein (cheese, egg, meat), 1 cup whole-grain cereal (shredded wheat, oatmeal, puffed rice; something with healthy grains like Uncle Sam's cereal, which has flaxseed), 1 cup milk or yogurt, and 1 fruit.
Lunch: 3 cups salad or 2 cups cooked vegetables, 1 tablespoon dressing, 3 ounces protein, 1 starch.
Snack: 1 fruit, 1 ounce protein.
Dinner: 3 cups salad, 2 cups cooked vegetables, 1 tablespoon dressing or butter, 4 ounces protein, ½ cup starch.
Snack: 1 fruit, 1 cup cereal, 1 cup milk or yogurt.

To figure out what kind of vegetables and salads, meats or proteins, and starches are best for you, I recommend getting the advice of a nutritionist who specializes in food addiction.

Beware: not every nutritionist understands eating disorders in regard to food triggers and possible food addiction, and many won't agree with the idea of eliminating foods. (This thinking likely stems from years of working with anorexia nervosa where most foods are considered "bad.") So your food trigger may be baked potatoes slathered in butter, sour cream, cheese, and bacon. You'll want to avoid those ingredients just as the alcoholic needs to steer clear of wine, beer, or liquor. But a nutritionist may loathe having you do so, pointing out the nutritional value in those things. This is why I can't stress enough it's not the diet itself that's important to the food plan, but the structuring of what and when to eat and avoiding your triggers.

What, then, can you expect from a good nutritionist? Whether schooled in food triggers and addiction or not, a nutritionist can help you develop a balanced plan right for your body size. Once you get the plan, you can take it to someone well-versed in overeating issues, maybe someone overcoming bingeing in recovery, for second opinions and additional advice and adjustment.

Every bit of care in this regard is worth it because you're developing an eating plan for your lifestyle. Listening to that lifestyle is essential too, because you're sure to find where one starch is good for one person at lunch, another person may feel deprived and need two. If you work in an office and pack your lunch or dinner, you may need less than one cup of a starch like rice, where the road worker needs more protein, maybe six ounces. Some people don't need snacks. Others work odd hours and need to make their meals in a different formation.

Eating healthy through the day will help keep your blood sugar stable, which reduces cravings. Also, the more you eliminate sugar and white flour from your diet, the more your cravings will decrease.

Of course, you knew sugar would come up again, didn't you? Let's look at it for a minute and then at some specific foods and ingredients to watch out for.

Seeing Sugar in Disguise

Because of its stimulating properties, eating no sugar at all is easier than trying to handle it in moderation. The most difficult part is trying to find what foods really are sugar-free, because sugar is hidden in so many forms, with so many different names, in so many foods and drinks. You have to learn to read labels and find out what to eliminate.

> **Because of its stimulating properties, eating no sugar at all is easier than trying to handle it in moderation.**

The Five-Ingredient Rule will help. Look at the top five ingredients listed in a food item. Don't zero in on how many grams of sugar are listed. It can be misleading. You can think a food might be okay because the grams of sugar are low, but when even the tiniest amount can trigger you, that food needs to go on the AVOID list. You want to remove the sugar from what you eat as much as possible. Look instead at the total list that orders ingredients from highest to lowest amount. Is sugar or a derivative one of the top five ingredients? Then this is an item to avoid.

To really assess a food's sugar content, familiarize yourself with these varying terms for it, so you don't end up eating sugar hidden by a different name:

Agave Nectar

Corn sweetener

Corn syrup, or corn
    syrup solids

Dehydrated/evaporated
    cane juice/syrup

Dextrin

Dextrose

Fructose

Fruit juice concentrate

Glucose

High-fructose corn syrup

Honey

Invert sugar

Lactose

Malt syrup

Maltodextrin

Maltose

Maple syrup

Molasses

Raw sugar

Rice syrup

Saccharose

Sorghum or sorghum syrup

Sucrose

Syrup

Treacle

Turbinado sugar

Xylose

If you're questioning honey, molasses, and dehydrated/evaporated cane juice/syrup on the list, don't. Some nutritionists say these sugars are healthier than cane sugar because of the way the body breaks them down in digestion. Yet they are still triggers and can do just as much damage to your food plan as a spoonful of the refined stuff, because they can get you going on a binge. I tried honey with my tea because a well-meaning natural foods person suggested it as a better alternative to saccharin. But honey was the equivalent of sugar for me. Sweetness was my trigger, so I ended up having tea with my honey. Artificial sweeteners can work the same way.

Rethinking Sugar-Free Sweeteners

There are many different opinions on whether or not to include sugar substitutes in your plan. Frightening as it is to say, you may not know until you try sweeteners for yourself. Developing the best food plan for you will be a process of trial and error. But if you can avoid substitutes, then do. Even the taste of sweetness, and often the foods the sugar substitutes are in, are triggers.

Deciding on Drinks

What you decide about sweeteners will probably affect the beverages you choose, and what to drink is as important as what you eat. So many of us are used to flavored and sweetened drinks, whether it means soda pop, coffee, or tea. Some food addiction professionals will tell you to avoid all three of these beverages because the caffeine in them stimulates eating.

Caffeine, by the way, can be a two-edged sword when you're wrestling with food triggers, dysfunction, and addiction. Because of its stimulant properties, caffeine can increase metabolism, energy, fat burning, and calorie expenditure. It can also stimulate hypoglycemia (when your blood sugar level is low enough to affect brain function), when your brain sends you hunger cues to fuel up and raise the blood sugar level.[1] So use caution with the trial and error of caffeine in your plan.

While you could go decaf with the coffee and stick to herbal teas, drinking water will help you even more. Your body is made up of 60 to 70 percent water, and no person can survive more than a few days without it. The American Dietetic Association found that just a 2 percent water deficit can result in a 20 percent decline in strength; the lack of water is the number one trigger of daytime fatigue; and in 37 percent of Americans, thirst is often mistaken for hunger.[2] That's why you need to drink at least eight glasses of water every day to replenish what your body depends on, plus to better metabolize fat, feel fuller, and improve skin tone. But what's a good way to achieve it?

- If you drink one glass first thing in the morning and three to four glasses by noon, you'll be halfway to your daily goal.
- Drinking a glass of water thirty minutes before every meal helps you achieve that feeling of fullness to help prevent over-eating, and will help your digestion.
- Fill a two-liter bottle with water first thing in the morning to drink by the end of the day, an easy way to see how much is consumed and how much more your body needs (regardless of whether or not you feel thirsty). If carrying a two-liter bottle seems awkward, use a half liter or 16.9-ounce bottle you fill and drink from four times over the course of a day.

If you're a juice drinker, things are trickier. Juice needs to be considered a fruit and should be measured, so typically half a glass equals one fruit. If your food plan allows only so much fruit, you may want to forgo the juice and opt for the actual fruit to satisfy your hunger.

Gum

Right. Gum is not a food—at least it shouldn't be—but it's often used to substitute for food, so it's worth mentioning. I used to abuse sugar-free gum. When I committed to a food plan, I wouldn't take a chance on eating a piece of cake or a bowl of ice cream. I knew these could trigger me to binge again. Gum seemed safer somehow. It's not always. I was chewing something sugar-free, but I still was putting something in my mouth to relieve stress, bring comfort, and help me cope emotionally. It was the hand-to-mouth behavior and way of coping I needed to change because once I gave in to feeding my emotions and spirit with something to chew or swallow, that in itself was a trigger and whatever I put in my mouth was never enough.

This is where diets go so wrong for those of us who are wired for triggers. The mantra of a diet is *replace unhealthy foods like sweets with something healthy like carrots and celery*. But a so-called healthy food can trigger you just as much as a sugary, fatty one when you're feeding something that has nothing to do with nutritional needs.

After years of not having any gum due to addictive chewing, I now enjoy freshening my breath without being addictive about it. I believe some of these behaviors were more a function of emotional dependency and working on the spiritual and emotional recovery enabled me to no longer rely on these behaviors.

Going with Grains: Bread, Cereal, and Pasta

Most food plans for people with food addiction or who binge and overeat start without any breads or pasta since grains can be addictive and tricky to navigate. It's just simpler this way—to stay away from the trigger foods and then gradually build them back into a lifestyle plan, if possible.

If you're already building in bread, cereal, and pasta, be aware that one of the great challenges is making sense of their labels. Look for whole-grain products to get the optimum nourishment from what you eat. An intact kernel of grain is made up of three parts: an outer coat of bran, an inner layer of germ, and starchy endosperm in between. When wheat is refined to make white flour, the bran and germ are stripped away, along with most of the grain's fiber, vitamins, minerals, and phytonutrients (which in the grain fight disease, and in your body help prevent disease and infection). So look for 100 percent whole wheat or 100 percent whole-grain products, and pick "whole foods" as much as possible.

This may seem alien at first, since so many diets have told you not to eat any grains whatsoever. Yet everyone needs to find grains that are healthy and won't trigger a binge—and different grains will work for different people. You're changing from a diet mentality to a sane and stable relationship with food. When you eat whole foods, you're more likely to be satisfied, and when you're more satisfied, then you eliminate physical hunger from the triggers to binge or overeat.

In fact, diet breads have fewer calories but aren't exactly nourishing. Look closely at products that say "whole wheat" or "multi-grain" as there may be whole wheat or grains in the product, but they may have been pulverized or refined and are right there along with mostly white flour. The reason white flour is so dangerous is because its starches break down quickly in the digestive tract and enter the blood stream as glucose, the kind of sugar that converts easily to fat. In fact, there's a saying, "the whiter the bread the sooner you're dead," because there's little nutritional value in white bread—it's made with refined flour, a process that strips most of its B vitamins and iron, then replaces them with chemical "enrichments." Because of the process, even bread labeled as "whole wheat" but containing "refined flour" in the ingredients can spike blood sugar levels faster than a candy bar, according to a Harvard Health Glycemic Index Chart.[3]

TRIGGER TALK

Getting Started

Deciding you are going to change how you eat can be overwhelming if you think change has to happen *en full* now. You don't begin a journey at your destination. Rather, you take one step and then another and another. So when you start to change how you eat and formulate a food plan, you start where you can, how you can, and the best way is to identify what you'll do first and then next, something like this:

- **This week** I'll stop eating sugar.
- **Next week** I'll cut out white bread and white flour pasta.
- **By week three,** I'll have figured out with help the best food plan for me.
- **By this month's end,** I'll have eaten on the food plan for one full week.

See how identifying the steps gets you to living on the food plan and finding freedom within thirty days? See how within two months you can be living better?

Now identify how your new eating plan will help you keep going forward toward complete freedom like diets or ways of

So even for bread brown in color, if the label starts with "enriched wheat flour," the product is not whole grain, no matter what is printed on the packaging. *Enriched* is the ingredient term to steer clear of.

Using the Five-Ingredient Rule for Fats

Another word and ingredient we're already prone to steer clear of is *fats*, thanks to our diet gurus. We watch the word and look for it in terms of how many grams of fat are in this food or that. But in an effort to avoid fat, we buy skim milk, fat-free half-and-half, nonfat

eating in the past never have—chart the positive steps you are taking in place of things you used to do, something like this:

What I Did Then	What I'll Do Now
Ate whatever, whenever I wanted	Cut out sugar and refined carbs
Starved myself and then binged	Stick to my food plan and times to eat
Changed what I ate with my circumstances	Read food labels
Bought whatever looked good for the fridge and pantry	Keep kitchen stocked with healthy foods

Keep your "Then and Now" chart in a place that helps you keep taking steps toward your goals. If you're really having difficulty, there are inpatient and outpatient treatment centers that can help you when you can't get started on your own. With time and help you can internalize all of this soon enough, and you'll be in a whole new place of eating and living—the Promised Land of Freedom.

yogurt, low-fat mayonnaise, and low-fat salad dressing. Yes, these items have lower fat grams, but that's not our greatest concern. We think we won't be triggered to binge on yogurt and condiments, but there can be sugar in these items to trigger us to go for more satisfying sweets, like a dessert—or several. Lower-fat salad dressings have a lot of sugar in them, for instance, which is more dangerous to us than the fat in them.

What to do?

Use the Five-Ingredient Rule when buying salad dressings. Make sure sugar is not one of the top five ingredients (greatest content) in the food. This limits your choices but you will find dressings that are tasty and sugar-free. Once again, don't be afraid if the choices available are high in fat. If you are no longer bingeing and are eating reasonable amounts, this really doesn't affect weight. Plus, our bodies need some fats. Eating a normal portion of food helps fill us. Then we don't have to worry about a dressing with seventeen grams of fat in a tablespoon, because the tablespoon of dressing is far healthier than the binges.

The New Relationship with Food

By this point, you may feel overwhelmed, like this food plan business is too complicated. It's true you can get as obsessive about a plan as you once were in feeding your triggers. You're creating a new relationship with food, and as in any new relationship there are questions. *How much time do we spend together? Where shall we meet? What does this all mean?*

The good news is you'll find all the time you once spent and wasted on food is now available for a new embrace of life. You won't miss the race to hoard snacks or binge in secret behind a closed door, or the moments wiping your mouth and brushing your front for any crumbs or evidence of overeating. You can spend newfound time on other things that really do mean more to you and help you pursue and live your dreams.

Tips like the following will help—practical things you can do, and guiding principles for this new relationship you're making with food.

Know Appropriate Portions

Rigid planning threatened to undo me. I couldn't live my life weighing and measuring every bite. I do think weighing and measuring have a time and place, and some people need to do this for years, maybe always. Others can weigh and measure at home, but not when eating out. I know some people who find success by bringing their scales with them, even to restaurants, events, and another's home, so they're certain not to overeat.

In the beginning, as Marianne mentioned, you'll probably find more rigid boundaries are better than looser ones, and then they shift. What helped me find my own lines in the sand was being able to easily eyeball right portions. I needed to do this so I didn't presume I was eating right. I could know for certain. Up to now you may not have done well in thinking on your feet, or at the table, about what choices to make. Learning portion sizes helps you be informed and plan ahead.

To ensure I wouldn't be looking for food between meals, wouldn't eat more than I needed at any given meal, and wouldn't have to feel guilty for overeating or fear gaining weight, I used the following gauges. Measures like these help because there are some foods easier to assess in portions than others. For instance, an egg is nicely contained in a shell so you know one egg is one egg, and most slices of bread are each about 1.41 ounces (or 40 grams). But how to know the right portion of a salad with various mixed greens or a piece of meat or cheese?

- **A two- to three-ounce portion of meat** is about the size of your fist. This is considerably smaller than what's served at many restaurants, which is more the size of a paperback novel—good to know so you can eat just half or a third and take the rest home.

- **A three- to four-ounce portion of white fish** is about the size of a checkbook.
- **A one-ounce piece of cheese** is about the size of a small matchbox or a pair of dice.
- **One serving of raw, leafy vegetables** is about one cup, and cooked vegetables are about half a cup. It's good to be aware many restaurants double these amounts in the portions served.
- **One serving of brown rice, whole grains, or mashed potatoes** is the size of half a tennis ball.
- **One-fourth cup of dried fruit** is about the size of a golf ball.
- **One teaspoon of butter or margarine** is less than the size of a thumb tip.
- **An eight–fluid-ounce container of yogurt, or cup of beans, or cup of dry cereal** is about the size of a baseball.

You can come up with more visuals like this as you work out your food plan. Take the foods you most incorporate in your meals and put them on a plate next to items you can easily associate with them—things you know the weight and feel of, that are familiar to you: a cell phone, a lipstick, a computer mouse, a postage stamp, a business card, a dollar bill, a quarter, your key ring to the car and house. As you learn what's representative, it may even help for you to snap some photos or write down these associations on an index card or key the information into a reminder on your cell phone for handy reference.

In time, you too will be able to eyeball serving to know the right portion size.

The Beauty of a Plan

Most of all, as you look at the right food plan for you, remind yourself how the structure will actually set you free from so many decisions you've wrestled with in the past, on what to eat and where to get more food.

You'll know what you're going to do and you can be satisfied, not deprived and hungry, as a diet will leave you.

No one ever starved with three weighed-and-measured meals a day, and neither will you. Stay the course with the structure and let these words ring in your ears because they are the sound of success: *Just stick to the plan.*

FIFTEEN

Eating Out While in Recovery

These times are trickiest of all. How do you navigate eating out and socializing when you're watching for all those triggers that can be on every menu and table? You can't always check out from such occasions. So much of when and why we gather together in our culture is to break bread—and down buttery popcorn at the movies, ice cream at the summer concert, and fast food on the go. Schedules, parties, vacations, dates, and appointments all convene over food. Must these times keep you from sticking to your plan?

"It's just so much easier to follow the plan at home, isn't it?" reflects Sharon, thirty-seven, one of my clients working on her triggers for a year now. "That's why in the beginning I tried my best to make my life fit around my plan. I needed to do that to get established in a new way of eating."

You'll find that too. Remember, one of the ways a food plan helps you is its structure of the amounts and types of food, and times for eating. Handling changes and choices will always present certain challenges until you practice a new way of eating enough so it becomes rote, like buckling up when you get in the car to drive. The day will come when you just do what's right without thinking, when you really are free. In the meantime, you don't want to put yourself in the driver's seat without the seat belt (and your safety device is following the food plan).

"Early on the change made me confused and overwhelmed and

oh-so-anxious," Sharon said. "At restaurants, I was tempted by all the yummy choices. I'd sometimes play games in my head: *Well, maybe it's okay if I just eat this when I'm out and not at home. Maybe I'm not really triggered by it.* When I traveled, I worried about waking up late: *I've missed breakfast, but it's not time for lunch—how does brunch fit?* If I was with a group of friends and colleagues and everyone wanted to go out to a fast-food place to eat, I thought, *Now I'm really stuck.* There's not much I can eat without being triggered. The problems overwhelmed me."

> **The day will come when you just do what's right without thinking.**

NAVIGATING THE CHOICES

It can take a while to get all of this straight. So many of these situations trap you into thinking you can never get free. Or as Sharon put it, "It felt humiliating at first to ask, 'Can we please find a different place to eat, some place with healthy food choices?' Or, 'Is it possible we could eat our Thanksgiving meal at dinnertime instead of three o'clock so I can follow my plan?'"

I found it difficult the first time I was invited to someone's house for dinner too. I wondered if it would be too rude to ask ahead of time what was to be served. When I did, I was presented with another agonizing question: *Is it even more rude to ask if my piece of chicken could be cooked without the sauce and breading planned in the recipe?*

Once, I was at a dinner party and encountered my worst nightmare. My gracious host was serving a famous dessert. I don't remember the exact occasion or the dessert, but I do remember how this dear woman I really did love kept pushing me to try a taste. "Just a little slice," she pressed. "Really. It's to die for—Grandma became famous for this. Besides, it's the holidays. Be kind to yourself. One little taste won't hurt."

To die for, I thought, as she kept insisting and all eyes around the table turned on me. *If she only knew the truth of that! Just a slice? Be kind to myself? One taste could take away every bit of freedom I've hard-earned. One taste would be the worst thing I could give myself!*

How to respond without having to talk about a trigger, or be unkind, or draw the attention to make a craving seem even worse?

There are ways and the guiding principle is to stick to your plan. The following tools will help get you through the desserts, restaurants, occasions for eating out—and even the truly gracious, but unknowingly bullying hostess who pushes Grandma's dessert.

IF YOU FAIL TO PLAN, YOU PLAN TO FAIL

Thinking through situations and thinking ahead is a huge step forward. This is part of not just making but keeping your food plan. You're preparing yourself, strapping on that seat belt, driving defensively through the choices and changes along the way. You're strengthening your mind and spirit to help when your body or emotions feel out of control.

This isn't an issue of willpower. You're not looking for determination to stick to a diet. You're *positioning* yourself to make good choices. You're *planning* the change you will make. You're *relating* in a new way to food and eating. You're *mapping out the steps* needed to avoid the triggers and the behavior that will drag you down and set you back.

A practical thing you can do then is to write on a card ideas for sticking to your plan. One client of mine, Leslie, forty-two, actually became her own coach, available anywhere at the push of a button on her cell phone. She had recorded a pep talk to herself with reminders of her plan, and could listen discreetly—and in a powerful way—to remind herself what to do.

Another client, Lindy, twenty-nine, found she needed help on the road too. A recruiter for a high-tech company, she traveled more weeks than not, and the business meals could be pushed to all hours and all kinds of places, from the drive-in to colleagues' homes.

"I needed something beyond my own power," she said, "beyond knowing what I needed to eat (and not) and when."

She adapted a prayer from Psalm 63 to keep as a text message saved on her cell phone. In moments at the table when she felt tempted to give into a trigger, she'd pull out her phone to read the message and remember God could hear, see, and fight for and with her:

> You, God, are my God, earnestly I seek you; I thirst for you, my whole being longs for you, in a dry and parched land where there is no water. I have seen you . . . and beheld your power and your glory. Because your love is better than life, my lips will glorify you. I will praise you as long as I live, and in your name I will lift up my hands. I will be fully satisfied as with the richest of foods; with singing lips my mouth will praise you. On my bed I remember you; I think of you through the watches of the night. Because you are my help, I sing in the shadow of your wings. I cling to you; your right hand upholds me. The addiction that wants to kill me will be destroyed; it will go down to the depths of the earth. It will be given over to the sword and become food for jackals. But I will rejoice in you, God; I will swear by the freedom from this addiction that you promise me, and I will glory in you, while the mouths of the cravings that lie will be silenced.

Sound dramatic? It's no more drastic than taking a leap away from your plan and going ahead and ordering what everyone else does, knowing it can trigger you. It's no more crazy than falling into so much shame over this that you think: *I've already fallen off the plan today, so I'll just eat this carton of ice cream and get back on things tomorrow.* Why would you give up all you've worked toward for one meal, one taste, one bad situation, when you can have a plan on how to get through a lifetime of such situations?

What to Do in Restaurants

There's nothing worse than opening a menu to all kinds of wonderful things everyone around you begins to order, and not one thing fits your food plan.

Linda, forty-nine, used to melt in such a situation. "I might as well have been the Wicked Witch of the West and the menu was Dorothy's bucket of water," she said. "It was like the plan I'd been following just disappeared. So I'd make a bad choice, then struggle to get back on track."

She didn't want to dread occasions that used to be fun, or cut off others, or drag them down. She realized she didn't have to—she could

- **know great restaurants to suggest.** Linda made a point to scout out restaurants in her area and places she traveled that prepared great choices, dishes and items that were sugar- and white-flour-free, that layered in flavor without the ingredients that triggered her. She found others often enjoyed finding these places too.
- **check out the menu ahead of time.** Most restaurant menus can be found online at their website or Facebook page and be accessed by a smartphone. You can think things over and choose carefully what to order before walking in the door of the restaurant. You can also call ahead.
- **change the *way* of looking at the menu.** Linda doesn't read and dwell on or agonize over everything listed. "Sometimes it limits options to two or three choices, but I know the kinds of proteins and starches in my plan. As I'm choosing, I ask myself not what will be the most tasty, but what can I enjoy that won't trigger me to overeat. I once heard it said you have to be willing to give up short-term pleasure for long-term happiness. It works for me." I hope you noticed Linda mentioned "what can I enjoy." Just because you're changing your relationship with food doesn't mean you can never enjoy it

again. You can savor healthy foods and flavor, and eat satisfying meals. Feeling deprived because you have to eat plain grilled chicken with steamed vegetables and a baked potato every time you eat out can lead you to the same frustration the diet mentality did. Learning to be creative, trying new flavor combinations that are not triggers, will keep you engaged in sticking to your food plan.

- **ask for something off the menu.** Many restaurants will accommodate and chefs are experts with spices and herbs, without the typical triggers of sugar, white flour, and fats. If you see there are only options like tired, old baked chicken and steamed vegetables, seek the chef's ideas on preparations minus what you're avoiding, or ask for special peppers and citrus to add flavor. "I'm not afraid to ask for 'without the sauce or breading or gravy' either," Linda said. "More restaurants are used to this and the wait staff won't bat an eye, nor others at the table. Then I can enjoy my whole day, not just one meal, knowing I've chosen freedom over a plan failure."

- **give some grace** if the options don't perfectly fit the food plan but are close enough and much more satisfying. For instance, maybe you're at a restaurant where the best choice for lunch is a salad that happens to have sweetened cranberries. You can pick out the cranberries, enjoy the salad with a sugar-free balsamic dressing, and be okay. More difficult is the barbecue restaurant your friends pick, where everything seems laced in sugar: the sauce, the coleslaw, the baked beans, even the pickles. You might do better enjoying a salad with the blue cheese dressing or the green beans with bacon and red skin potatoes or corn on the cob, than eating a plate of barbecue slathered in brown sugar sauce. Or, better, you can see if unmarinated meat, possibly rubbed in spices only, can be cooked over the mesquite without the sauce to get the satisfying grilled flavor without the sugar.

Confronting Buffets

You probably know too well the sayings about buffets: you can't get enough of everything. That's the problem, right? Even if you've already determined to avoid the buffet, but your family, friends, and colleagues are going, you don't have to marginalize yourself. You don't have to let the buffet have power over you. You can

- **fill up on your goals before going.** Remind yourself there will be a whole table before you with temptations within reach, so think how much better it is to hold on to rather than hand over your recovery.

- **be okay with not getting your money's worth.** All-you-can-eat situations usually cost a little more because it's assumed you'll go back for more. Don't. To put the old Nike slogan in reverse, just don't do it. It's easy to fill up, thinking you're going to get what's coming for your dollar, but this can cost you peace of mind. So what if you paid twenty-five dollars for vegetables, a simple protein, and a normal portion of starch? If it keeps you to your plan, that is worth more than whatever is spread before you.

- **look on the bright side of the variety.** Look for all the things you can eat. Don't linger before the things that you can't. As you move on to the things right for you, remind yourself how much you're learning and how far you've come to stick to your plan. This can be another step to celebrate rather than an event to mourn.

Handling Parties, Special Occasions, and Holidays

The challenge with events is being at the mercy of the schedule and types of food available. At receptions, like for a wedding or retirement, appetizers can float around like little birds that light on your shoulder and whisper "eat this" or "try me." For holidays, there can be an endless parade of family-favorite foods, most of them high fat and sugary—and irresistible. At a dinner party, you might not be served the meal until nine o'clock at night.

Just this weekend I attended a Bat Mitzvah. The service ended at noon, and then it took an hour to get to the country club. Appetizers didn't appear until one thirty, and lunch wasn't served until nearly four o'clock. I'd had breakfast at seven a.m., and knew nutritionists advise not to go three to four hours without eating because you get hungry, your blood sugar dips, you're tempted to forage for the closest thing, you overeat, and there go the triggers.

What to do in any of these situations?

- **Plan on appetizers.** You know they're going to be there and the times for the meal could lag. So keep the appetizers to the equivalent of the snack you'd normally have between lunch and dinner. Only now, you're going to have the snack between the breakfast you ate and the "lunch" that's coming, no matter how late in the day lunch arrives. This is kind of what dieters do with exchanges, only you're not dieting. You're not making this your practice. This is your exception, your way to manage a special event.

- **Choose appetizers like a snack**—vegetables, fruit, some kind of protein like nuts (almonds and pistachios are lower in fat, if nuts are not a trigger food) or a deviled egg, something adequate enough to satisfy and as equivalent to a snack as possible. Remember, you're not going to make a meal of the appetizers because a meal is coming later, and if the appetizers are trigger foods, you won't die to skip them and wait. The idea is to make the best possible choices without crossing your boundaries and without making the event a bigger emotional issue driving you to those triggers.

- **Carry a snack in your purse or car,** a packet of almonds for example, in case there aren't appetizers and the meal is going to be late. You can enjoy the snack in your car before arrival at the event, or in a quiet corner. Think of this as your Agent 007 secret weapon, protection so you won't be in a position to overeat.

- **Assess the meal and edit your plate.** If you can find out ahead of time what will be served, then discreetly ask a server or host if it's possible to have something without the sauces or breading or whatever triggers you. If you can't know ahead of time, take stock of the meal when it arrives and edit what's right or not: Is there too much protein or starch? Is there too little of something you need? Try to do the best you can to eat what you need. You'll live, if the potatoes aren't as much as you usually eat. You won't die, if there aren't enough vegetables. This is okay. It's a special event. It's not going to be your norm. Give yourself some grace without crossing those boundaries.
- **Think of a day of food celebrations, like Thanksgiving, as just another Thursday.** Instead of focusing on all the free-flowing food all day, stick to your food plan. Remind yourself how much better you'll feel caring for yourself this way than falling into a food coma.

Dealing with Dessert

This may sound impossible right now, but you *can* pass on dessert.

Janine, twenty-eight, wasn't so sure at first. But after following a plan, she has realized it's true. "I've been not eating desserts for three years and, honestly, the cravings have disappeared. I know it sounds like a miracle, and maybe it is. Others are amazed to see me turn down those 'must haves' everyone else 'must have.'"

Can you expect such a miracle? Can finding freedom from desserts really be so clear-cut?

It wasn't so simple for me. I grew up eating dessert after every lunch and every dinner. Learning how to end a meal without dessert was a real challenge, and took a series of phases. First, I tried filling the gap with some other treat, a sweet drink like coffee or tea with a sugar substitute. Then I determined to lose all kinds of emotional ties to food. I saw this after-dinner drink as a dependency. So I began to abstain from my after-dinner sweet drink with a ritual of brushing my teeth. The very act of cleaning my teeth, and the fresh taste of the toothpaste, gave me a ritual closure for ending the meal. Some people try another ritual like chewing sugar-free gum.

Eventually, I found I could walk away from a meal without dessert, the after-dinner sweet drink, and even brushing my teeth until later. It's the retraining of the brain, I believe, and also your new life, the freedom from food triggers like Janine experienced. You're embracing all that's good, so it's less tempting and you have less craving for what brought on all the shame and madness with desserts all those years.

TRIGGER TALK

"But Other People Can . . ."

How many times have you left someone's company, where they downed something fabulicious while you or someone you love with food issues silently sipped water, then fumed: "It's just not fair. Why do I have to avoid so much? Other people don't. Why do I have to plan ahead or watch everyone else get all that's good? Why can't I just eat like normal people?"

Well, other people? Everyone else? Normal? What's "normal" anyway?

Remember: The person who's not fighting sugar as a trigger may be deathly allergic to strawberries. The man who eats a juicy bacon cheeseburger may have heartburn and fat build-up that's killing him. The skinny lady downing a huge bowl of pasta with the cream and cheese sauce might be bulimic and already thinking how to rid her body of every bite she's eaten. You don't know what issues others face with their food.

You do know you can be triggered to binge and overeat, and

Things that help:
- **Focus on the people, not the plates of dessert.** "Someone long ago urged me to engage more in conversation than get caught up with what was being served. This was the best advice," Janine said. "I began to realize it was friendship I wanted more than the food anyway."
- **Veer away from the vices.** I found it easier at first to simply excuse myself from the table as dessert arrived and everyone else was indulging. It was too difficult for me early on to watch and not have any myself. If you're at a large party, it's easy. You just head to the restroom and chat with someone

you're on the road to freedom from food. Who knows what road they're on?

When you think of these choices as stops on a journey to freedom and away from the pits of food triggers, you don't really want to detour anyway. A normal person's cheesecake could be the deadly breakdown to your physical, emotional, and spiritual well-being. Even a bite of everyone else's dessert could trigger the deadly addiction cycle and keep you from the freedom you're gaining. Other people's indulgence is not your dream and truly your nightmare.

Esau in the Bible learned this. He traded his birthright and father's blessing for a bowl of stew (Genesis 25:29–34). One bowl for a birthright. Even if he traded for a whole pot of stew or stew every night for a week, was it worth his birthright? No more than one bite of cheesecake is worth your dreams and your freedom.

When those feelings come of what everyone else seems to get that you don't, I tell myself and my clients the simple truth: Get over it or it will get you. This is your life. Let others have their just desserts.

along the way there or back. If you're at a more intimate gathering, you can excuse yourself to make a phone call, check something in your car, offer to help clean up the dinner or serve the coffee (but not the sweets), and prepare some decaf or herbal tea for yourself. Often someone else finds it nice to get away and share the dessert avoidance with you, admiring a piece of art in the hallway or book on the coffee table, stepping out for a moment of fresh air.

- **Smile, say little, and hear less.** I've found it easier to not explain why I'm refusing dessert. Too many people don't understand that food triggers work like alcoholism. They don't really believe in sugar addiction as a serious issue and devastating problem—they consider it more a diet matter. It's just easier not to talk about it with a whole table or room of people and all eyes on you. Of course, sometimes you can get backed into having to respond, like I did with the gracious hostess who kept pressing me for a taste or a tale. I eventually had to respond, "No, I really can't have even a taste." But still I didn't go into detail about it at the table. I said, "I can tell you more about it later." You can say, "I have an issue with desserts." This can be uncomfortable, so I remind myself: *What others think doesn't matter. This is what I have to do because dessert can be devastating for me. No one else really has to understand or believe it. I do.*

- **Distract yourself and others.** Lindy told me she learned to be a master of deflecting such scrutiny. She simply changed the subject far away from food and often to favorite films or books, as most everyone has something to say about those things.

SIXTEEN

Build a Winning Support System

When Sue, forty-five, and I met in January, she looked great but confessed she felt terrible. She had been losing weight—thirty-nine pounds over the last three months. The long hair she used to hide behind had been cut into a style that made her seem younger and showed off her sparkly brown eyes.

"You look stunning," I greeted her. "How are you doing?"

"Three sizes smaller than I've worn in fifteen years," she said, plucking the side of a slimming pencil skirt. "Such a wonderful moment for me when I tried on these new clothes at Christmas and they fit, and I liked what I saw in the mirror. But . . ." Her smile faded. "Honestly? I feel terrible."

The old feelings can still lurk. "What's happening?"

Before Christmas, Sue had been invited to a big soiree. Marian, a new friend from work, had talked for weeks about this annual party she always threw. She had lots of other single friends and promised, "My friend Dave will be there, and he's adorable. You two would hit it off!"

Sue, never married, wished for something like that. She'd waited all her adult life to meet the right man. After nearly twenty years of battling a food addiction, she'd finally made changes these last four months to feed her spirit rather than her cravings. She felt ready to live to the fullest.

Before she even got to the front step of Marian's place, though, all her hard-earned self-confidence began to wane. Then the door opened to a room full of beautiful people laughing and chatting, holding wine glasses and plates of hors d'oeuvres.

"You look fantastic," Marian whispered into Sue's ear as she slid out of her coat. "Dave is excited to meet you." Marian nodded toward a tall man on the far side of the room.

Sue's heart leapt. He was handsome, but it wasn't that—he had a calmness and a kindness in the way he was fixed, listening, to the people around him.

Sue laughed nervously and said she would just take to the kitchen a fruit and cheese tray she'd brought. In the fifteen seconds it took to make her way there, slipping through the clumps of guests—all beautiful, none familiar—the same old patterns began. She felt scared. Unsure. *What if nobody talks to me and I'm left alone in a corner? I'll feel like a fool. Dave won't want to talk to such a loser.* Anxiety burned from her racing heart, down her arms to her fingertips. She thought she might drop the plate she'd brought. She felt light-headed, her knees weak as she stepped through the swinging door to the kitchen. She steadied herself against the counter, covered with trays of sliced meat, sacks of chips, boxes of crackers, plates of fudge and cheesecake.

Sue nudged aside some of the stash to make room for her plate, and felt the old hunger. She didn't know a soul in the scary room she'd just moved through, but here were all kinds of beautiful and familiar. A tray of thickly frosted mini-cupcakes called to her. *Cream cheese on red velvet. Mint on chocolate. Caramel on pumpkin. Maybe just one. No, they're just bite-sized. Maybe two. Maybe . . .* She hesitated a second, then grabbed the tray and headed back to the laundry nook. She was alone with the enemy, her old self who threatened all the progress she'd been making. Even as she tasted the frosting of a first cupcake, she knew she didn't need it.

Yes, I nodded when Sue paused in her story.

"I needed a friend instead," Sue said.

"Yes." But not just one. Two. Three. Maybe five.

What It Means to Live Free

You can be like Sue and find yourself breaking free from old patterns, making progress. Then, boom! Something happens to bring you right back to where you were: a situation, a person, the sight or scent of a food you used to rely upon for comfort.

Sue found herself facing all three. She was someplace unfamiliar and feeling anxious about connecting with anyone. She was on the cusp of meeting someone she already hoped to like (and whom she hoped would like her back) yet was terrified of rejection. Then she found her anxious self alone with a plateful, albeit miniature versions, of the go-to food she used to scarf a carton at a time in an effort to assuage disappointment.

She needed reinforcements, and quick. It turned out she knew that with even the first taste of frosting. She put down the cupcake and picked up her phone to call Karen, a new friend from the support group they had both just joined for people fighting food addictions. But Karen was out of town, in an area where her phone didn't have service. She never even got Sue's voice mail until days later.

Meanwhile, Sue stood in Marian's laundry room, the buzz of the party growing on the other side of the kitchen door, just like her anxiety. So Sue succumbed. With no one to help talk her through her fears, she sought comfort in the cupcakes, which were familiar and gave pleasure for just a moment. She ate at least six before the swing of the kitchen door made her put down the tray, wipe her mouth, and pretend like she was on her phone. Then she rejoined the room, loathing herself the rest of the evening. The moment's pleasure never lasted. She knew that. She'd been living that truth and had victory upon victory. Now, relapsing into old, bad behavior brought new pain. She couldn't even think about getting to know Dave or others, she was so fixed upon hating what she'd just done. The evening was a misery.

"I kept thinking people could tell I'd just stuffed my face with all those cupcakes," she said. "I kept biting my lip, trying to hide a crumb or bit of frosting that might be there to give me away. I'd meet one of Marian's friends and instead of really hearing what they were saying, I'd be thinking the whole time: *Did they see me? Do they know? Maybe they're going to call me out on what I've just done, what I've been doing all my adult life.*

Living free from our addictions doesn't mean we never have temptations again, that we're never presented with another crucible moment. It doesn't mean—presto change-o!—we're "fixed." Healing doesn't mean being perfected.

Living free from our addictions means we're stronger. We know more. We've come through a fire. It means we know with the skills we've learned, choices we've practiced, and faith we've built, we can face the fire again and come through stronger, better, and more refined. It means we know enough to see when the flames are too high or too close and we're in danger of getting burned unless we have a shoulder to lean on or strong arms to carry us through. It means sometimes we need a friend, and since that friend, for whatever reason, may not be there, we need another and another—and one more, and even one more.

WHEN MORE IS BETTER

There's a Bible proverb that says one may be overpowered, and two can defend themselves, but a cord of three strands is not quickly broken (Ecclesiastes 4:12).

I love that because it's the same with people as with cords. When you're on your own, you're vulnerable. You can slip and need help to get up. One friend can steady you from slipping. But two friends can pick you up when you fall. Three can carry you. When you have even more friends? You're armed, ensured for success.

The one friend you call, like Sue's Karen, may not be available. So you need another person on your list for support, and in case that person is unavailable too, you need another. You may need five or even ten friends you can call in your own cupcake moment.

TRIGGER TALK

The Hundred-Pound Phone

There will be moments when you know you need help, but picking up the phone seems next to impossible. Your cell might as well be a hundred-pound weight. Your pride might as well be the thousand-pound cup of coffee you cannot put down. You're thinking you want a double cheeseburger with bacon and a large fry and maybe a chocolate shake. But what you really need is a slice of humble pie.

You need to swallow that pride and call for support. You need to know it's okay. Being vulnerable isn't a weakness. Reaching out is a strength. Calling for support before and after a potentially triggering event can be the smartest single act you do. You want to think through beforehand what you're going to do and get through it—dealing with all your crazy family members and food at the same time, for instance. Then, afterward, you want to decompress with someone about how you made it through, an accountability call that helps you settle down. In this way, support is God's gift to us because it gets us through the hard places when we don't have the strength to take one more step ahead.

Thinking *ahead* is exactly what can help. Ahead is the longer-lasting feeling of joy that you overcame a temptation. Ahead is the sweeter truth that you can do this. Ahead is the you who is stronger, healthier, more free. Ahead is the help of a friend just a call away.

So when you think you can't lift the phone, ask yourself this: Could I do it if my life depended on it?

You know the answer: it does.

Living free from an addiction can, indeed, take a village. Or, as God puts it, with many counselors, there is victory (Proverbs 11:14).

Sue found that out when she reached out for help and Karen wasn't there. No one but God can be there all the time. So He gives us helpers who can be front and center when we need them most.

But, right. How many of us have even one friend who would pick up our phone call at two in the morning? Or who would leave a job for us in the middle of the afternoon to help us out of the fast-food drive-through? Or who would drive across town to keep us from the cupcakes? Or ditch their holiday plans to talk us away from the visions of sugarplums dancing in our heads?

For most of us, there are only so many people we'd be so vulnerable with anyway. So I hear you when you say, "Five friends I could tell anything, call on anytime, from anywhere? Really? Not even possible."

But it is possible. The friend you call when you need support is not necessarily the friend you go with to shop for shoes or watch a movie, or meet for coffee. The friend you call in your cupcake moment may be more of an acquaintance, someone who doesn't even know your favorite color or the latest book you're reading. But they know your biggest fear, your greatest food temptations. They understand the surge of anxiety, the pull of a craving, the loathing of indulgence, and the shame of succumbing. They get it because they too have been there, done that. They may be someone you've just recently met, like Sue's Karen from the food-addiction support group. They want the same thing you do: the freedom that ultimately satisfies more than the trap of one moment's pleasure or relief. They are the friends who

- **understand** and identify with what threatens your ability to live free;
- **believe in you** and want the best for you;
- **know how** to be discreet and keep private what you confess or do in vulnerable moments;
- **offer safety** by keeping to the road of recovery as well; and

- **don't judge** you as "bad" for the temptations and allures you experience, and celebrate what's good ("you called!") and each step of progress that you make ("you just got through this!").

The List

When I say friends like this are keepers, I mean it in the most literal way. You want to keep an actual list: their names, their contact information, and the best times to reach them, or (easier, perhaps) when they are not available. In fact, it's good to identify who can be on your morning list and who is best for evening, who is near your home and who is by your office, who can listen with their kids in the next room and who can actually come to meet you without having to get a sitter for their children.

It means you must weigh your list with what you've learned about when you're most vulnerable: the situations and people, places and foods that might trigger you. Are you especially at risk when you're going out to dinner with friends? Who can you ask to be on standby for a call? Do you know Thanksgiving week is going to be a time for petitioning God for help resisting all the food mixed with family angst? Is there someone in the family you can put on your list?

Think of the list as your support staff, your assistants, and right hands. When your own hand is tempted to grab something to stuff in your mouth, friends on your list will offer you their hand instead. They'll help you talk about food, feelings, God, and anything else you need to process.

Sue admitted if she'd had such a list at Marian's party, she would not have given up when Karen's phone rang and rang, or when the call finally went to voice mail, or when she was standing at the counter covered in beautiful, tempting finger foods and desserts. Those cupcakes might still be on the platter in the kitchen, she said. She would have been so much more free to mingle, and maybe she would have been more open to Dave, who did end up asking her out a week later, but admitted he wasn't sure she liked him because she seemed a little closed and distant.

The list really can offer that kind of power—power for you to resist a binge because you're freaking out over your first job interview in a long time, or you're so far behind on a project that taking a break to pig out is a temptation, or you've got a big test or a funeral or a dozen other difficult things. So, using the guiding criteria above, who in particular goes on your list?

- **The overcomer.** This is the person who has had success with eating and living sanely. Think of the person talking about freedom in everyday life. The myth is that the person handling food well is the overcomer. But you can find people who have lost weight in all kinds of diet programs, and they may be thinner but they're still not free. I'm talking here about the person living a full, abundant life, the person who is feeding their whole self, body, mind, and spirit, and understands how to manage emotions and feed your soul.

- **The encourager.** This is the person who understands the fear of failing, who speaks out against it with words you need to hear more than you need the doughnut. Think of the person who talks about the worth of trying and keeping on and persevering. This person isn't necessarily always smiley and perky, but accepting and empathetic, warm and caring.

- **The forgiver.** This is the person who has probably messed up a lot and knows the power of starting again. Think of who talks of redemption and mercies, the person who will remind you each next second is your second chance, and everything can be fresh and new from right now.

- **The coach**. Who do you know who is part strategist, part cheerleader? Think of the person who can talk you out of your crisis moment and give you moves to make, who provides motivation for the next step in your process toward freedom from cravings.

As you develop your list, keep it where you don't have to think twice about who to call when a batch of brownies or bag of chips threatens to cry out your name. The list needs to be as much a go-to thing for you as food was once. It needs to be keyed into your cell phone's contacts, on a slip of paper tucked into your purse or pocket, and posted inside a cupboard or on the refrigerator.

The point is to have the list always at hand. When you're in a crisis, you won't have the energy or reserves to think of how to reach who you want to call. If the first person you call doesn't pick up for whatever reason, you need the next name and number right there, and then the next, and a next. Your list may grow over time as you find more friends and supporters to add to it because—think about it—how many times are you tempted to use food for comfort in a day or a week? It's at least half the number of people you need on your list.

It Can Take a Village

There are other supports, beyond the five-plus friends who need to go on your list—supports you call upon regularly, intentionally, with planned effort and commitment, not just at random and in crisis. There's nothing wrong with needing support in crisis. This is what help is all about—you ask for it when you need it, and you can't always plan when that will be.

But where your list of friends is a life preserver to reach for when you feel yourself going under, these additional supports are like the lifeboat that carries you from the beginning. To think you can go it alone or with just the list is like jumping ship in the middle of the Atlantic with just a life preserver, thinking you'll make it ashore healthy, whole, and happy. You won't, no matter how hard you try, how strong you are, how resilient you are becoming. There are too many triggers like sharks, too many high-sweeping emotional waves, and too many harsh elements to batter your spirit.

It's not a failing. It's just being human.

To make sure you chart a steady course, plan on at least some of these additional helps:

Seek Out Support Groups

You can't underestimate the power of a good support group. Those who have experienced the pain and shame of food addiction will understand what you're going through and what you need like no one else.

> Those who have experienced the pain and shame of food addiction will understand what you're going through and what you need like no one else.

It doesn't mean finding a group is easy. Finding one to best serve you can be tricky. Some groups are stronger than others, and a few emphasize food plans more than addressing the total person of body plus mind, emotions, and spirit. Some groups are large and the company of many can energize you. Other groups are small and the intimacy may help you more. So much depends on your personality and the leaders and members of the particular group.

I found the groups who made literature available to be helpful, especially when they had us study it together to learn recovery principles. I was also helped by groups where people in recovery didn't just talk about food plans and weight loss, but shared personal experiences of overcoming.

A good place to start is with the free nationwide groups:

- **Overeater's Anonymous (OA)**, online at www.oa.org, with phone meetings 24/7 and podcasts
- **Anorexia and Bulimia Anonymous (ABA)**, online at http://aba12steps.org/, with free literature and advice
- **Celebrate Recovery**, online at http://www.celebraterecovery .com/, also with free advice

Keep in mind it's good to try out several meetings before assuming a particular group is good or bad for your needs. Marcy was thankful she had been to some good OA meetings in her hometown before she went away to college. Because she had experienced a group where people were successful, she was not completely thrown by the lack of success in the group near her college. If her first OA experience had been the one at school, she said she would never have returned. Marcy knew she needed to venture out and explore different opportunities until she found the support she needed. She had to put some effort into it, but eventually she did find an excellent support system not too far away.

Find a Nutritionist

This may come as a surprise, but finding a nutritionist with a background in food addiction treatment is not as easy as you think. Just because someone understands food doesn't mean they understand addictions.

What you want primarily, regardless of background, is someone who will help you beyond the recommendation to abstain from sugar and white flour. Others in your support system can help you tweak what you get from your nutritionist to make sure you avoid triggers.

Consult a Therapist-Counselor

As you begin to face your food issues, the triggers and consequences, you're going to come nose-to-nose with a host of feelings, not all of them good or pleasant. Like a bully, these feelings won't budge and they're going to be intense. They'll frighten you and probably those around you, especially those closest to you. Change is never easy, nor welcomed. Confidantes and family members can't always help you navigate the changes either. In fact, they may have contributed to the long-denied feelings you now face, so their interests may conflict with yours.

You're going to need certified help, someone schooled and experienced in standing up to emotions like abandonment and rejection, self-loathing and shame. A certified therapist is, by the root definition of their title, someone who makes it their profession to care. Not all therapists are certified and some have education and some don't. But a good certified therapist will listen to you, care, show you how to express yourself in healing ways, be well versed in addiction and recovery groups, and work out a recovery plan—and those are the criteria to look for. Not all eating disorder professionals ascribe to the addictions model, so that is something to ask about and consider too.

Seeing a Psychiatrist

If the emotional distress becomes too great, you're going to need more than therapy. You may need medication, which only a licensed psychiatrist or a medical doctor can prescribe, to ease the emotional intensity. Be aware, then, this isn't a first tier of support. It's a second tier, when you've tried therapy and found the emotions are so debilitating it's better to take something to alleviate the distress than abuse food and keep the addiction going. In choosing a psychiatrist, look for someone who:

- **spends an adequate amount of time** with a client and asks targeted questions to enable a diagnosis and treatment plan
- **listens, really listens**, and conveys concern
- **understands medications** and their safety issues and interactions. This means looking for someone who will stop medications if they haven't worked after a reasonable trial, or will lower doses or change medications if there are unreasonable side effects, and who communicates understanding of how the risks of medicines may outweigh the benefits
- **is hopeful, optimistic, and encouraging** that your life can be better and you can manage your issues
- **is flexible enough to try another treatment or approach** (and another and another) if the first ones don't work
- **seeks consultation when the going gets rough** and will see you when you are in distress. Sessions every three months may be fine for someone who is doing well, but "come back in three months" isn't reasonable if you are not doing well or need a medication change. A good psychiatrist will find alternatives, such as phone contact, in such cases.

- **communicates with other physicians and therapists**, if necessary
- **is respectful of your time** by returning phone calls and running generally on time. Making you wait fifteen minutes frequently may be okay, but consistently running two hours should be addressed.

Being a Friend to Yourself

Perhaps one of the greatest pegs in a winning support system is the one you never think about, the one you've taken for granted and advantage of, ignored, used, and failed to value. It's *you*, and the strength God designed within you. He designed you to be of faith, hope, and strength.

But for too long, you've not been kind to yourself, you've not valued yourself enough to say, "Enough! Enough of the binges and overindulgence. Enough of the time wasted with food, enough money wasted on diets, enough energy wasted on trying to hide the overeating and the weight gained. I can live better than this. I can feel better."

The truth you now know is: you can.

Now is the time then to know yourself, and like yourself. Here's how:

- **Learn about who you are**, all your likes and dislikes. You've used food so much to satiate your greatest desires you may not know what they are anymore. Maybe you know you like creamy desserts more than cakey ones. But what's your favorite genre of music? Have you really explored and listened to many different kinds? What fragrances of nature fill your soul most: piney woods or salty sea and sand? Do you love cozy nooks on rainy days best or sunny meadows? Determine to unlock a passion. When Julia Child was a new bride in 1948, she moved with her husband, Paul, to France and stumbled upon her lifelong passion of cooking.[1] She was just looking for something to do while Paul was at work with the United States Foreign Service, so she took a cooking class at the famous Le Cordon Bleu cooking school, and it opened a new world to her. She trained under several master chefs, wrote the first wildly popular English cookbook on French cooking techniques, hosted a television show, and began a new life as a beloved gourmand. There may be something you've never done or known about yourself because your time has been spent thinking on food so much. Now is your time of discovery, to become more *you*.

- **Treat yourself like you would a friend.** Be kinder and gentler with yourself. You would never tell a friend how fat he is or how stupid she's being. Don't talk to yourself that way either. Whenever a self-denigrating thought enters your mind, replace it with a good one: *I am bringing something great to the world today. I'm glad I'm here. I love the world and myself.*

- **Become more self-sufficient.** That means developing relationships out of conscious choice rather than desperate need, looking at where you can rely on yourself to handle finances or management of your household rather than someone else. Is there one area in your life where you can take back management of something?

- **Enjoy your own company.** You don't always have to turn to someone or something else for fun, interest, and fascination. You can love a solo morning walk, reading by yourself in a café, creating fragrant gardens, making your own line of handmade gift cards. Take a class or sign up for a weekend workshop on something that interests you. Make a date with yourself on a regular basis to try new things. Listen to many different genres of music and note which ones you really like.

- **Be your own support group.** Write down things you know you're good at and remind yourself of them. You may be the most generous person, or a great mom and wife, or a hard worker. What would you say God enjoys most about you? Your wry sense of humor? The way you laugh? Celebrate your great qualities and when you're feeling beat up by food issues, call in your inner cheerleader: *I am wonderfully made* (Psalm 139:14).

THE GREATEST FELLOWSHIP

You can have the best food plan, a support group, a ready list of friends to call in crisis, even medicine to control consuming emotions. But there will be cracks between all those things in your life, places where those people and things can only do so much. A friend can steer you away from the cupcakes. A food plan can keep your stomach from growling and give your body the fuel it needs to function. A therapist can help you face and deal with your hurt or feelings of self-loathing. But who helps feed your soul? Who reminds you of God's mercies and His work in you that you may not always see?

God's people will give you a pillar of support too, acting as His hands and feet in this world. In a faith community you will find people who encourage you, pray with and for you, and help you see God's provision, care, and love.

Not everyone you find in a church will understand food addiction issues. But you'll find many people who rely on faith know what it means to need saving and spiritual support, and to rely on mercy. They can help you find and remember God's promises to

- **give you His goodness** here and now (Psalm 27:13);
- **do a new thing** in you (Isaiah 43:19); and
- **make a hope for you and a future** (Jeremiah 31:17).

If you don't already belong to a church and want more information about differences in denominations as well as how Protestants differ from Catholics, check out *The Unauthorized Guide to Choosing a Church* by Carmen Renee Berry. With humor and a conversational, not theological, approach, Berry looks at the differences between Catholic and Protestant churches, and denominations within the latter. The book begins with a self-survey to identify what you believe about God, what churches best fit your beliefs, and where to start looking for the faith community where you can grow, worship, pray, learn, find encouragement and support, exercise your faith, and nourish your soul.

In the end, nourishment for the soul is what Sue said she craved most. She developed her list of five friends and was able to call and get help the next time her anxiety met a cupcake that hollered for her attention. But it was fellowship and prayer that gave her the strength to walk away from the cupcake.

"If I need a friend who doesn't pick up, I am learning to summon the strength now to call the friend who's always there," she says.

And the best friend of all?

God, who really can help you go with a prayer, not a platter.

SEVENTEEN

It's Not Just
about the Food

Now you know a diet and a food plan aren't just about the food, and wellness and freedom aren't just about dealing with your emotions. Success in reaching your health and weight goals are as much about an action plan and dealing with your emotions and behavior, and surrendering your spirit to God's power after you've done all you can do.

The important thing is you are changing not just your eating patterns, and, with that, your fitness and shape, but your whole way of living.

LIVING FREE IS A LIFESTYLE

That means there are additional practical things you can do to keep yourself trigger-free. These things include everything from your daily schedule to how you arrange where you live—things you can manage right now, with just what you have, right where you are.

Make Substitutes

I'm not talking about food exchanges here as much as filling up the places food used to occupy, places including your time, activity, and attention. You've spent a lot of time with food: thinking about it, going to get it, and eating it. You've maybe had dates with food every night or weekend in front of your television (which probably set off even more triggers with all the food ads).

Now that food is relegated in structured amounts to structured times, what do you do? The possibilities are endless! Several clients have told me the things they now do to replace the bowls of ice cream and high-fat snacks:

- **Take a walk** in the fresh air
- **Read** a book
- **Call or visit** a friend
- **Start a project**, like needlework or knitting
- **Clean up**—unload the dishwasher, fold laundry, iron, or organize files
- **Write** letters
- **Groom or cuddle** with the pet
- **Reach out** to someone in need—and get out of thinking and looking at yourself
- **Explore** a new hobby or area of interest
- **Listen** to music
- **Relax**! It really is okay to take some time for being at peace in whatever way you find it, like maybe soaking in a tub of sea salts or sitting on the porch listening to the birds sing or on a city bench watching people.

An important caution is not to sit in front of the television, which can be a huge trigger in and of itself. Most of us zone out when watching TV, and we're idle, sometimes even bored. It's too easy to reach for food in such moments. I made it a rule to never watch television without the company of others, which kept me from a binge.

Put Things in Writing

Somehow commitments you've already made in your head become even more powerful when put on paper. The very act of writing can seem more formal, like forging a contract to keep with yourself, both a reminder and an accountability statement that includes

- **the specific foods** you will eat;
- **times** you will eat and how much; and
- **who to call** for support, help, and physical accountability.

Keeping this document visible on your computer, phone, calendar, refrigerator, or mirror can help even more. The visual aid will remind you to stay the course or celebrate steps you're making each day. Reading it aloud will help you think even more seriously on your commitment.

Surround Yourself with Help

As important as the food is for success in getting healthier, the people around you, day in and out, are just as significant. That means, in addition to the support system you're building:

- **Let those closest to you know you're working to change**. You don't have to go into great detail. Just mention generally what you're trying to avoid, and ask for their prayers and encouragement.
- **Ask for a no-food-gifts policy.** This will stop tempting and trying situations where people typically bring candy or cupcakes to your desk or doorstep. Most people do things like this to be caring, not realizing they've just created an agonizing situation.
- **Find people who can help you process aloud** the issues and changes you'll face, especially during those first three weeks of abstinence from your trigger foods. Because trigger foods can be addictive, you may feel like an addict in withdrawal from a substance. By day two or three, you may feel anxious and experience cravings. By day four, you may find yourself restless and frustrated. Days five and six, you can get angry. By days seven through nine, you may flip-flop between moments of anxiousness and clarity. It may be day ten before you get the sense of getting better and that you can do this. Through the changes, friends and family can give you

an important listening ear and support. You can tell them, for instance, *I need to dine with someone tonight so I stick to my plan.* Other times, you may need the presence of role models, people who have also struggled with overeating, but now have a track record of success.

• **Find a shopping buddy for when you need to stock up at the grocery store.** It's easier to feel triggered when you're alone, and walking through delis or bakeries and down grocery aisles of food, which can be a gauntlet, especially during the holidays with all the festive goodies prepared and ready to sample.

Clean House

Starting fresh means clearing away all past temptations from your kitchen, pantry, refrigerator, cupboards, and wherever else they're kept. As good as it is to get rid of things, it's equally important to replace them with healthy foods on your plan. So for all the snack crackers and ice cream you give away (and ingredients, like one client tells me of refrigerated pie crust and cans of Eagle Brand condensed milk triggers), stock up on healthy foods like vegetables, nuts (if they're not a trigger food), and fruits. You want to enable your new way of eating as much as disable opportunities to stray.

The key here is you're not looking for food to have around—you're trying to stop the bad behavior. This requires some work, organization, planning, and shopping, and you'll immediately find it worth the attention and energy. Having what you need to stick to your plan keeps you from indulging in something that can trigger.

Stay Constant

Whatever your structure, stick to it. When you're consistent, there's little need to obsess, worry, or fuss. You don't keep changing things, which can set up opportunity to fail. You know what you're doing with food, and that's freeing.

Easier said than done?

Not necessarily. Remember all the research about how you can retrain your brain? Staying constant helps you form new habits. You don't operate out of the myth consistency comes from willpower, which is like a pool that drains through the day and isn't the issue with triggers anyway. You operate out of structure. You establish boundaries and create rituals and practices. You make the loop essential to forming a new habit by repeating it: you know your stable context, follow your routine, and experience a reward. Your reward is feeling better in every way—physically from the junk food and the weight, emotionally from the guilt and shame

> When you're consistent, there's little need to obsess, worry, or fuss.

TRIGGER TALK

When You Love an Overeater

The greatest thing someone can do for a loved one trying to eat better and live well is to come alongside with not only encouragement but helpful action. That means: keep the junk food, sugar and sweets, high-fat snacks, and refined carbohydrates out of the way. Things you can do:

- **Clear out the large boxes or containers of trigger foods** from the cupboards, drawers, and house.
- **Eat healthy** with your loved one. If you're going to indulge in foods that trigger someone, do it somewhere away from them.
- **Attend a support meeting** to learn more about it.
- **Accept and support** the need to attend meetings or make calls for encouragement and advice.
- **Don't try to monitor** what's eaten, but don't ever hush talk about it, both of which can perpetuate the shame that accompanies eating and addiction issues.

of overeating and bingeing, and spiritually from the madness of the addiction—by forming new relationships to replace the ultimately unfulfilling one with food. To stick to your routine, it helps to

- **start simple.** You can't expect to completely change in one day. But you can expect to change this minute, this meal, this day. Remind yourself: *This is one step. This is what I can do now. I will stick to my plan for breakfast, and now for lunch, and now at dinner. I can be free this meal, this morning, this night, each day at a time.*

- **cook ahead.** If you fear not being able to spend so much time weighing and measuring at meals through every day, and haven't yet mastered being able to eyeball right portion sizes, prepare meals ahead of time. This works well for those who hate to cook too—get it over with in one fell swoop. Make lunches and dinners for the week and store them in the freezer (so there's no temptation at hand), setting out just what you need one day at a time. If you fear temptation as you cook, all the picking and tasting, invite a friend over to perhaps taste things, help cook, or simply for accountability.

- **keep reminding yourself to stay structured and specific.** These are the ingredients for success. When you don't stray, and stay on target, you overcome. It's that simple. Of course, life doesn't always make us think recovery is simple. Things do not always go as we best plan. Times will come when you can't prepare your food like you need—what then?

You Can Do This

As much as you plan and follow the plan, there may be times you blow it. You get off the plan, you cave in to a trigger, and disappoint yourself.

You can still move forward.

Every morning, every minute, after blowing it is a chance to get back on track. Some of the greatest successes came from the refusal to quit, the determination to keep going. Even if you fail ten times, success can come on the eleventh attempt. The next time you try can be the time you succeed.

Don't let yourself give up because you gave in. Take heart. There is a way of eating that is satisfying and livable. The key is changing your thinking as much as changing your eating. The power to change comes through an entire process that involves this food plan, but doesn't revolve around, begin with, or end in it. Keep focused on living better and better, and changing the patterns of how and what you eat, and what it will mean over time—and that can be sooner rather than later!

Don't let yourself give up because you gave in.

I know you care about the weight. We all do. But when you care as much about your whole self and know that when you stay structured, stable, and constant, the weight will come off—even better, so will the burdens that have driven you to put on the pounds in the first place.

Writing a New Story

I will give thanks to You,
for I am fearfully and wonderfully made;
Wonderful are Your works,
And my soul knows it very well.
—PSALM 139:14

I will always remember the day I stood before the mirror at our front door, fluffing my hair and touching up my lipstick, and a woman in my family hurried past, mumbling over her shoulder, "I don't know why you even try."

I was sixteen, not even out on my own, and was already stopped from becoming all God intended. Her crushing comment in passing, something she probably doesn't even remember today, triggered years of grief. I tried to soothe the worthlessness and hurt I felt with sweets, but was rewarded with pounds instead. I ate again and again for momentary pleasure, and it just triggered me to keep on eating. In the end, shame weighed me down to the point of giving up on myself.

Thank God, He doesn't give up on us.

Thank God, He gives us every reason to try.

Thank God, He's made a way for us to succeed even when we fail.

God promises us we can overcome even when we've fallen or been put down (sometimes by our own selves) for even trying. He promises us mercies new every morning (Lamentations 3:23), and that He can do what we cannot.

Those mercies are like a bank account He has set up in your

name with unlimited access and funds. So you gave into a trigger tonight? Just draw from the account now for mercies to start fresh. You overate at the church potluck and then went home and ate again? No worries. You've got unlimited mercies to begin again. You were

TRIGGER TALK

A Divorce Decree

Dear Trigger,

My addiction, my replacement lover, most reliable friend, secret-accepting partner, space filler, painkiller, mind numb-er, escape hatch. I'm terrified to say good-bye to you. We've been married so long now. You're such a large part of me. Huge. Enormous. You've made me big in the worst way. I'm afraid to let you go. I mean, honestly, the big part of me that you've built up—all the fat, the extra weight I've tried to lose but keep putting on, has been with me so long, I'm not sure who I'll be without it. What will be left of me? The parts I've been too ashamed for anyone to see, because you've whispered in my ear so long how undeserving I am to be anything else, with anyone else, without you by my side, in front of my face, in your grip?

You've really made me who I am . . . and it's not what I want to be anymore. You've led me to the most shameful places and been behind my worst actions: the lying and hiding, stealing, desperation, judgment, and criticism. Come to think of it, you've been the one who told me to binge, isolate myself, retreat from others, avoid stuff and deny, rage, despair, and feel hopeless.

That's the part of you I don't want anymore. I'm tired of the pain, the hurt, the put-downs, the way you demand my attention and money and love. I need more than you've given me, which hasn't been much: humiliation, embarrassment, loneliness, poverty in spirit and pocketbook from always chasing after you.

bored while home alone and ordered one too many pizzas and binged on all of them? Okay. You blew it. There's still more mercy from God than there could ever be pizzas delivered.

This doesn't mean you can bank without regard on grace, or try

Who do you think you are, anyway, demanding the very best of me—my time, my attention, and years of my life—with nothing in return?

We've tried separation and it's never worked. You don't even meet me halfway. You want all of me, whole hog, pigging out, blissing out with you until I'm bloated, depressed, and wiped out. You don't really care if I give up other things to spend time with you or money on you. You are so selfish. You take any good memories I've had, any dreams I hold. You would rather I sit alone with you in the dark or behind a closed door than build real relationships and ventures.

So here's the thing: we're done. I'm so over you. It's time for you to pack your bags, take all your friends, all the snacks and desserts and fast food and candy wrappers, and go. Scram. Oh, I know there will be times I really miss you, times when I'm sad and vulnerable because I'll think of those momentary pleasures with you. But what a master of deception you've been, a wielder of illusion. You never really cared about me and those few happy moments with you never did last and never did mean anything good. So stop lurking and skulking around my life. Stop the taunting and teasing. I'm going now and we're done.

I'm being pursued by someone new, and, you know, I like it. Freedom is the real deal, and offering me what you never could: peace of mind, more fitness, sanity with eating, real relationships.

Yes, Freedom is giving me what I never had with you.

A life.

to stop what triggers you to overeat. "God forbid!" as the apostle Paul said, "Shall we sin because we are . . . under grace? May it never be!"

The grace and mercy are what get us out of the cycle of living in shame and continuing to abuse food, causing more shame. So when you've got unlimited mercy, you've got all you need to keep going. You can be filled with God's grace instead of grievous amounts of food. You have God over your shoulder, not just passing by, but repeating again and again

- *I know you* (Psalm 139);
- *You are My workmanship and I made you for good works* (Ephesians 2:10);
- *I think you are wonderful* (Psalm 139);
- *You are My treasure* (Exodus 19:5);
- *I designed you to live abundantly* (John 10:1–10);
- *I want you to have the desires of your heart* (Psalm 37:4; Philippians 2:13);
- *You can do this, and what you cannot do, I will* (Ephesians 3:20; 2 Thessalonians 2:16–17);
- *I will never stop doing good to you* (Jeremiah 32:40).

Just as some people's words can stop you, God's promises can start you again. His mercies can trigger you to keep going, keep trying, and start living.

If by the time you read this page, you haven't accepted His gift, you can do so now. You can say *hello* to life abundant. You can say *enough* to food abuse, even though you've been on intimate terms with it, taken it on vacations and to visit family, spent many a night in its company, asking it to hand over the cookies and pass the Ding-Dongs.

Now is the time to finally say good-bye.

Write a Dear John letter to all your triggers: to the foods, emotions, and behaviors you've binged on and that enticed you to stay in an unhealthy place. This is your chance to declare your release. Say what you won't miss and why you're leaving the prison where the triggers would keep you. Tell why you choose freedom instead. Remember how you met, the first time you cycled into abusing food or fed an emotion and unhealthy pattern of behavior: What did you like in the beginning? What was the attraction that kept you coming back? What went horribly wrong? When did you notice it? What's wearing you down now? What moment did you know this affair was over?

End your letter with a prayer. Ask God to take every trigger, and to go with you into a new life, where you fill up on Him rather than food.

He will do it. In the same passage where He promises new mercies, He assures you cannot be consumed and He will be your portion (Lamentations 3:22–24). He will give you what you need and then one helping more and one helping more.

And one more.

THE TRIGGERS LIST
YOUR QUICK GUIDE TO FAST HELP

ACKNOWLEDGMENTS

When I began my recovery journey in 1981, I never expected to be in the place I am today. Many people helped me get here, greatly impacting my personal recovery and professional development. Though I may not mention each one by name, my gratitude is deep for every single person along the way.

To the wonderful people who were there for me at the start of my recovery and through it: Thank you. I've been blessed by each of you who gave me time and energy, listened to my carrying on about my troubles, wiped away my tears, held my hand, walked me through tough times, laughed with me, encouraged and believed in me, shared faith, prayed with me, and taught me how to live a healthier, better life. I wouldn't be here today without some of you most precious people who, just because you had been there too, put heart and soul into helping me when I was a big mess. Thank you for being there to save my life, and then helping make my life worth living.

To my recovery buddies and the few therapists in my life: Thank you. Diane Langberg, especially: You may have come later than the rest, but you have influenced me the most. Your own example has helped make me a woman who wants more of God and less of me. Thank you for not giving up on me, and believing in me, even when you know the truth about my messiest parts.

To my spiritual family: Eternal thanks for you, a community of people who have helped me grow spiritually. I searched high and low for you, and you are my spiritual home, the place where I can safely develop my faith and learn about God—and without God, there would be no recovery, no *Food Triggers* book. I love you in a very special way.

To my husband, David: My biggest thanks. I can't thank you enough for never giving up on me, always urging me ahead, and continually adding support in a million ways from doing the small administrative tasks to giving incredible financial provision.

To my beautiful, precious daughters, Danielle, Jessie, Arielle, and Jordan: Deepest gratitude. Thank you for hanging in with me all the years of my doctoral program, for the millions of little details I have needed your help with, and for patience during insanely busy seasons. Above all, I can never thank you enough for being my best cheerleaders, for believing in me and encouraging me through thick and thin. I love you each in a special, unique way. You make my life immeasurably better.

To my parents: Thank you, of course, thank you for always being there to help and encourage.

To many friends: I count myself blessed by you, who have been there to support me, whether it's by just checking in or listening to long whining sessions over the challenges, or with your presence at breaks in the day; and prayer, encouragement, input on details, pats on the back. My colleagues, so many of you fit into this category. There is nothing more wonderful than people who care enough to ask about things or take the time to provide the needed encouragement to carry on. In particular, what a difference you make in my everyday life: Goldie, Sara, Marlene, Rachel, Margaret, Marji, Chris, Lynn, Debbie, Virginia, Cheryl K., Faith, Jason, Roxanne, Kathy, Cheryl S., Terri, Michelle, Bob, and Tim.

To some great professionals—speakers, counselors, and authors—who have become very special and important to me as friends and colleagues: Big thanks, especially to Tom Whitman, founder of Life Counseling Services, where I have been able to develop a practice using the addictions model for nearly twenty years. Thanks to Amy Feigel and Jennifer Cisney-Ellers, who have become wonderful friends helping me connect with the right people at the right time. Thank you for tremendous support, Mark Laaser and Dwight Bain, who each have mentored and coached me to develop my skills as a speaker and author—your expertise and encouragement has been incredibly helpful. Thank you to the American Association of Christian Counselors (AACC) and Tim Clinton for making a place where counselors can develop and share their expertise with each other, and for welcoming the addictions model for food addiction treatment despite some controversy over it in the counseling field.

Special gratitude to professionals who have been laboring in our field as pioneers using the food addictions treatment model. Ours has not been an easy road. There has been great controversy, and we have been a small voice in a sea of people disagreeing that food can be addictive. Anne Katherine and Kay Sheppard: Thank you for being some of the first to write, in the eighties, about food addiction, thank you for breaking the ground. Phil Werdell and Mary Foushi: You have truly committed your lives to creating awareness and helping those suffering from food addictions. Marty Lerner: Your successful, awesome residential program, Milestones in Recovery, has been treating food addiction for many years, and your treatment methods work. Theresa Wright: You are a brilliant nutritionist and dear friend to whom I am grateful for leading the way in teaching people in food addiction recovery how to manage eating correctly. To the folks at Yale's Rudd Center: You are engaged in research and public policy regarding food addiction, and I am so grateful. Your research has validated something recovering communities have known, and you have helped to make that reach for help more likely for more people.

To Michelle Medlock Adams: Thank you for crafting a proposal that helped open the door for this book to be published.

To those directly involved in making *Food Triggers* happen: So much thanks. First to the wonderful people at Dupree Miller: You were willing to take this idea to publishers, and I am honored beyond words to have you on my team. Jan and Shannon, through this process you have provided wisdom, support, and practical help to see everything through. Thank you for all you have done, and for believing in this book. Lacy, you are amazing. I am so blessed to have you in my corner, working to make this project a success. Thank you for being there for all the countless details, and thank you for your all-around support.

To Jeanette Thomason: You are a gift from God. I can't thank you enough for how you put your special touch on my message and made it come alive. I am a psychologist and needed a storyteller, and, you brought out the emotion of the real people whose stories are shared.

To the Worthy Publishing team: My sincerest thanks and deepest gratitude to be included in your group of great authors. You have been far more incredible than I could have dreamed. Each of you have been helpful in different ways, and all with excellence in your area of expertise. So thank you, Byron Williamson, Jeana Ledbetter, Morgan Canclini, Dennis Disney, Alyson White, Jennifer Day, Diane Vanderford, Sherrie Slopianka, and the many others I've not yet personally met but who have made this book happen.

I'm grateful for the additional help of media trainer Ellie Scarborough and publicist Pamela McClure, and am amazed at how each of you made such an important and meaningful difference.

To Daniel Decker, who came on board to create a wonderful new website along with promotional materials: Thank you for insight and awesome ideas, and I am blessed to have you on the job. To Michael Barrett: Thank you for creating an awesome book trailer. And to Terri and Bob Gillespie and Arielle Epstein: Thank you for helping with the video shoot.

Most of all, my greatest thanks, God, to You, from whom comes all good things, from the beginning, to the end, and through every detail of this process. Your unfailing love, grace, wisdom, and provision, go on and on forever.

Preface

1. "Eating Disorders Among Adults – Binge Eating Disorder," National Institute of Mental Health, http://www.nimh.nih.gov/statistics/1EAT _ADULT_RB.shtml; "Eating Disorder Statistics," National Association of Anorexia Nervosa and Associated Disorders, http://www.anad .org/get-information /about-eating-disorders/eating-disorders-statistics /; and James I. Hudson et al., "The Prevalence and Correlates of Eating Disorders in the National Comorbidity Survey Replication," Abstract, *Biological Psychiatry* 61, no. 3 (February 1, 2007): 348–358, National Center for Biotechnology Information (PMC1892232), http://www.ncbi.nlm.nih.gov/pmc/articles/PMC1892232/.

Chapter 1: Willpower or Wiring?

1. Caroline Davis, "From Passive Overeating to 'Food Addiction': A Spectrum of Compulsion and Severity," *ISRN Obesity* 2013, Article ID 435027. Twenty pages also online in review at http://www.hind awi.com/isrn/obesity/2013/435027/, and in full at http://dx.doi.org /10.1155/2013/435027.

2. "Overweight & Obesity" chart from the American Heart Association, 2009, online at http://www.heart.org/idc/groups/heart-public /@wcm/@sop/@smd/documents/downloadable/ucm_319588.pdf.

3. Luca Passamonti et al., "Personality Predicts the Brain's Response to Viewing Appetizing Foods: The Neural Basis of a Risk Factor for Overeating," *Journal of Neuroscience*, January 7, 2009, 43–51.

4. Ibid.

Chapter 2: The Chemistry of Triggering

1. Two important studies detail the brain chemistry similarities in people with food addiction and people with addictions to other substances: N. M. Avena, Pedro Rada, B. G. Hoebel, "Evidence for

Sugar Addiction: Behavioral and Neurochemical Effects of Intermittent, Excessive Sugar Intake," Abstract, *Neuroscience & Biobehavioral Reviews* 32, no. 1 (January 2008): 20–39, http://www.ncbi.nlm.nih .gov/pubmed/17617461; David Mysels and Maria A. Sullivan, "The Relationship between Opioid and Sugar Intake: Review of Evidence and Clinical Applications," Abstract, *Journal of Opioid Management* 6, no. 6 (November/December 2010): 445–52, http://www.ncbi.nlm .nih.gov/pmc/articles/PMC3109725/.

2. Ibid. Also: Kitta MacPherson, "Sugar Can Be Addictive, Princeton Scientist Says," Princeton University, December 10, 2008, http:// www.princeton.edu/main/news/archive/S22/88/56G31/index.xml ?section=topstories.

3. Ibid.

4. Ibid.

5. Avena, Rada, and Hoebel, "Evidence for Sugar Addiction."

Chapter 3: Know Thyself

1. Ashley N. Gearhardt, William R. Corbin, Kelly D. Brownwell, "Yale Food Addiction Scale," Yale University, New Haven, CT, 2009. Available online at http://www.yaleruddcenter.org/resources/upload/docs /what/addiction/FoodAddictionScale09.pdf.

2. Laura Sanders, "The Brain Set Free," *Science News* 182, no. 3 (August 22, 2012): 18–21, http://www.sciencenews.org/view/feature/id/342 559/description/The_Brain_Set_Free; Massachusetts Institute of Technology, "MIT Researcher Finds Neuron Growth in Adult Brain," December 27, 2005, *ScienceDaily*, http://www.sciencedaily.com /releases/2005/12/051227111212.htm.

Chapter 4: The Science of the Spirit

1. Several articles amass the wealth of study on how faith helps healing, builds immunity, and benefits your thinking and physical abilities. These two comprehensive news features point to the array of research: Jeffrey Kluger, "The Biology of Belief," *Time*, February 12, 2009, http://www.time.com/time/magazine/article/0,9171,1879179,00.

html; Gery Wenk, "Religiosity and Neuoroscience: Does the Absence of a Serotonin Receptor Lead to Spirituality?" *Your Brain on Food* (blog) *Psychology Today*, August 2, 2010, http://www.psychologytoday .com/blog/your-brain-food/201008/religiosity-and-neuroscience.

2. Cell biologist Bruce Lipton, after pioneering studies at the University of Wisconsin and Stanford University, coined the phrase "the biology of belief" in his book by the same title that examines how faith brings about health: Bruce H. Lipton, *The Biology of Belief: Unleashing the Power of Consciousness, Matter, and Miracles* rev. ed. (Carlsbad, CA: Hay House, 2008).

3. Andrew Newberg and Mark Robert Waldman, *How God Changes Your Brain: Breakthrough Finding from a Leading Neuroscientist* (New York: Ballantine, 2010).

4. Corrie ten Boom, *The Hiding Place* (New York: Bantam, 1971); Corrie ten Boom, *Tramp for the Lord* (New York: Jove, 1986).

5. Pamela Rosewell Moore, *The Five Silent Years of Corrie ten Boom* (Grand Rapids: Zondervan, 1986).

6. Newberg and Waldman, *God Changes Your Brain*.

7. Barbara Bradley Hagerty, "Prayer May Reshape Your Brain . . . And Your Reality," *All Things Considered*, radio broadcast, National Public Radio, May 20, 2009, http://www.npr.org/templates/story/story.php ?storyId=104310443.

8. *Standards for Life* (Bristol, TN: Christian Medical and Dental Associations, n.d.), http://www.faithandhealthconnection.org/wp-content /uploads/2007/11/the_faith_and_health_connection_cmda_standards _for_life1.pdf. This publication of the Christian Medical and Dental Associations lists dozens of respected studies that show faith does help health and healing.

9. Brother Lawrence, *The Practice of the Presence of God* (1958; repr., Grand Rapids: Revell, 1967).

10. Sindya N. Bhanoo, "How Meditation May Change the Brain," *New York Times*, January 28, 2011. Online: http://well.blogs.nytimes .com/2011/01/28/how-meditation-may-change-the-brain/?page wanted=print. The *Times* blog post refers to the findings of Britta

K. Hölzel, James Carmody, Mark Vangel, Christina Congleton, Sita M. Yerramsetti, Tim Gard, and Sara W. Lazar, "Mindfulness Practice Leads to Increases in Regional Brain Gray Matter Density," Abstract, *Psychiatry Research: Neuroimaging* 191, no. 1 (January 30, 2011): 36–43, http://www.psyn-journal.com/article/S0925-4927%2810%2900288-X/abstract.

11. Mark Wheeler, "Evidence Builds That Meditation Strengthens the Brain," March 14, 2012, *ScienceDaily*, http://www.sciencedaily.com/releases/2012/03/120314170647.htm.

Chapter 5: Looking for Love in All the Wrong Places

1. Sandra Boynton is an American humorist, songwriter, children's author and illustrator, who has written and illustrated more than forty books for both children and adults, as well as more than four thousand greeting cards and four music albums.

2. Dawn French, BrainyQuotes, http://www.brainyquote.com/quotes/quotes/d/dawnfrench263651.html.

3. C. S. Lewis, *The Lion, the Witch, and the Wardrobe* (1950; repr., New York: HarperCollins, 2002).

4. Janet Greeson, *It's Not What You're Eating, It's What's Eating You: The 28-Day Plan to Heal Hidden Food Addiction* (New York: Pocket Books, 1990).

Chapter 6: What Is Eating You?

1. The adage became the title of the bestselling book by Sylvia Boorstein, *Happiness Is an Inside Job: Practicing a Joyful Life* (New York: Ballantine, 2007).

Chapter 7: Stinkin' Thinkin'

1. Daniel G. Amen, *Change Your Brain, Change Your Body: Use Your Brain to Get and Keep the Body You Have Always Wanted* (New York: Three Rivers Press, 2010). His theories of ANTs, automatic negative thoughts, are peppered throughout the book, especially chapter 13, "The ANT Solution."

2. Alvin Powell, "Alcohol Abuse after Weight Loss Surgery?" *Harvard Gazette*, July 30, 2012, http://news.harvard.edu/gazette/story/2012/07/alcohol-abuse-after-weight-loss-surgery/. The roundtable of Harvard neuroscientists, psychologists, and surgeons was generated by initial research at the University of North Dakota Medical School's Department of Clinical Neuroscience, published as a May 1, 2006, paper for the Journal of the American Medical Association: Ninh T. Nguyen et al., "Result of a National Audit of Bariatric Surgery Performed at Academic Centers: a 2004 University HealthSystem Consortium Benchmarking Project, Abstract, *Archives of Surgery* 141, no. 5 (May 1, 2006): 445–450, doi: 10.1001/archsurg.141.5.445.

Chapter 8: It's All Peace and Love

1. Stephanie Paulsell, *Honoring the Body: Meditations on a Christian Practice* (New York: Jossey-Bass, 2002), 33.
2. Jane R. Hirschmann and Carol H. Munter, *When Women Stop Hating Their Bodies: Freeing Yourself from Food and Weight Obsession* (New York: Fawcett, 1995).
3. James 5:7–18 tells how prayer and changing your thinking, being patient and enduring results in goodness—how even the prophet Elijah, "with a nature like ours," prayed and believed for years for a thing to happen, and it did.
4. Ibid.
5. James 5:11–16.

Chapter 9: Walking the Minefield

1. "Princess Diana's Anti-Mine Legacy," CNN World News, September 10, 1997, http://www.cnn.com/WORLD/9709/10/diana.angola/index.html.
2. Diana, Princess of Wales, "Responding to Landmines: A Modern Tragedy and Its Solutions," Gifts of Speech website (keynote address, Mines Advisory Group and Landmine Survivors Network seminar, London, June 12, 1997), http://gos.sbc.edu/d/diana.html.

Chapter 10: Tackling the Trigger Strongholds

1. *Alcoholics Anonymous*, 4th ed. (New York: Alcoholics Anonymous World Service, 2002).

2. "Make Me an Instrument of Your Peace" or "The Prayer of St. Francis of Assisi" can be traced back to its first publication in 1912 in French in the magazine *La Clochette* (The Little Bell) as an anonymous prayer and then in the January 1927 Quaker magazine *Friends' Intelligencer* (Philadelphia). It is widely attributed to the thirteenth-century St. Francis of Assisi.

Chapter 11: Sweet Surrender

1. The moral tale about a boy and a snake that turns on him is told in the legend and lore of many people, including the Cherokee, Seneca, and Hindu. A version of it can be found online at http://www.indigenouspeople.net/snake.htm.

2. Muhammad Ali became the first and only three-time lineal heavy-weight champion of boxing, earning the Golden Gloves champion-ship in 1959, an Olympic gold medal the following year; and all his bouts in the 1960s—the majority by knockout. In 1999, he was named "Sportsman of the Century" by *Sports Illustrated* and "Sports Personality of the Century" by the BBC.

3. Portia Nelson, *There's a Hole in My Sidewalk: The Romance of Self Self-Discovery* (Originally published, Los Angeles: Popular Library, 1977; Hillsboro, OR: Beyond Words, 1994). The story of choos-ing a new course is actually a poem called "Autobiography in Five Short Chapters," a few lines of which begin each of the book's five chapters.

Chapter 12: Do What You Can and Let God Do the Rest

1. In Colossians 2:2–3 the apostle Paul encourages us that there is wis-dom, truth, and assurance in knowing God's will, and yet His ways still remain a mystery. Psalm 77:14 says, "You are the God who works wonders; You have made known Your strength among the peoples." In Isaiah 45, the prophet acknowledges that God does hide Himself at

times, that He is a mystery, and yet He always delights in being found and, indeed, chases us. God tells us in Habakkuk 1:5 to be astonished at how He works for us: "Because I am doing something in your days—you would not believe if you were told."

2. In the first study to examine what the public thinks about people with an addiction to food, research from the Rudd Center for Food Policy & Obesity at Yale found that the notion of food addiction could increase the stigma already associated with obesity. The findings were reported in Megan Orciari, "Are 'Food Addicts' Stigmatized?" Yale News, February 5, 2013, http://news.yale.edu /2013/02/05 /are-food-addicts-stigmatized. For the full study, see Jenny A. DePierre, Rebecca M. Puhl, and Joerg Luedicke, "A New Stigmatized Identity? Comparisons of a 'Food Addict' Label with Other Stigmatized Health Conditions," Yale University Rudd Center for Food Policy & Obesity (New Haven, CT: Routledge Taylor & Francis, 2013), doi: 10.1080/01973533.2012.746148.

3. Cassius Clay, who later changed his name to Muhammad Ali, delivered the line about how he would win all his fights because he would "float like a butterfly, sting like a bee" in what's come to be called his "I Am the Greatest" speech, first broadcast on the February 24, 1964, episode of the CBS television series *I've Got a Secret*, hosted by Gary Moore.

Chapter 14: Developing a Food Plan

1. Angela Ogunjimi, "Does Excess Caffeine Prevent Weight Loss?" *LiveStrong* (blog), December 22, 2010, http://www.livestrong.com /article/340997-does-excess-caffeine-prevent-weight-loss/#ixzz2 .blefBYFu.

2. Susan M. Kleiner, "Electrolyte Envy: When Water Alone Isn't Enough," http://www.hylytes.com/documents/Kleiner-Electrolyte Envy.pdf. Kleiner is the owner of High Performance Nutrition, a consulting firm in Mercer Island, Washington, and the author of seven books, including *The Good Mood Diet*, *Power Eating*, and *PowerFood Nutrition Plan*.

3. "Glycemic Index and Glycemic Load for 100+ Foods" chart, Harvard
   Health Publications, Harvard Medical School, http://www.health
   .harvard.edu/newsweek/Glycemic_index_and_glycemic_load_for
   _100_foods.htm.

Chapter 16: Build a Winning Support System

1. Julia Child, *My Life in France* (New York: Alfred A. Knopf, 2006).

Introduction: My Story

1. Everyone has a story about their triggers. What do you relate to most in Rhona's personal story?
2. What books, diets, plans, or things have you tried so far for encouragement and help?
3. Have your food issues been called other things—depression or anxiety, for instance? What names have you used for your food abuse or heard others use? Addiction? Overeating?

Chapter 1: Willpower or Wiring?

1. If shame were a person, how would you describe him or her— the way of operating, the relationship qualities, the personality and mannerisms?
2. How does shame come to you and how does it leave? When does shame seem most powerful?
3. How does it make you feel to know any issues you have with binges may have to do with the way your brain is wired and not with willpower at all?

Chapter 2: The Chemistry of Triggering

1. What are your impressions of an addict? Does any of that apply to you with food?
2. In what ways has trauma or anxiety triggered your overeating? Can you talk about it? If not, write it down to keep private and pray upon your thoughts.

Chapter 3: Know Thyself

1. What do you think of the new research that says you can retrain your brain not to respond to triggers?

2. What are three specific things you would like to retrain in your brain?

Chapter 4: The Science of the Spirit

1. How have you thought about (or not) the help of God and of your faith in Him with regard to your food triggers?
2. When have you witnessed or experienced the biology of belief or belief affecting well-being?
3. When has prayer affected your health, and how? When have you seen or experienced prayer having seemingly no effect?

Chapter 5: Looking for Love in All the Wrong Places

1. What emotions, moods, or situations have most driven you to reach for food?
2. Our culture seems to celebrate turning to food as a way of dealing with a bad day or situation. Where have you seen signs of this? What do you think when you see these signs?
3. How have you been able to distinguish a physical hunger from an emotional one? How do they seem the same? Describe both the physical signs and emotional signs of hunger you've experienced.

Chapter 6: What Is Eating You?

1. What was the first time you remember bingeing or being triggered to overeat? How old were you? Where and what happened?
2. How did you relate to food growing up? Were you a picky eater (if so, with what foods and why)? Were you deprived of certain foods? What foods were always around for you or restricted as special or only for special occasions?
3. Once you began to binge, how did you typically do it? Where, with what, for how long?

Chapter 7: Stinkin' Thinkin'

1. What are the most recent negative thoughts that have looped through your mind? Are some of these thoughts reoccurring? How often? When and in what circumstances do they tend to occur?

2. Think about a time you had one negative thought after another pile up. Discuss with a trusted friend or reflect in your journal about how one thought led to another, how it changed your behavior before the bad thoughts (from what, to what—what happened?).

3. How do ANTs (Automatic Negative Thoughts) feel as they come upon you? How are you left feeling by them? Describe physical changes when your mood and perspective shifts.

4. Do you think you've switched addictions or dysfunction with food to something else? What compulsions or preoccupations have arrested your attention now that you've taken it from food? Identify these things in your journal and think on how to take them captive too.

5. What excuses have you made in the past so that you could binge?

Chapter 8: It's All Peace and Love

1. What are the anxious thoughts that plague you most? List them on a sheet of paper. Now offer them to God. Burn or bury or tear up the paper as you release them to His care. Pray to receive His peace in exchange.

2. Do you think it's true that how you think of yourself affects how you carry yourself or appear to others? How do you think you appear at an all-time low in a binge cycle versus a time you feel your best? What is different?

3. Think of people who have a great presence despite their size. What do you like about the way they carry themselves? What makes them attractive physically, spiritually, emotionally? List the qualities you see as positive, good, and beautiful.

4. What is the most difficult thing about learning to love your body?

Chapter 9: Walking the Minefield

1. What are your go-to reactions when you're frustrated by a difficult person or situation? Do you automatically get angry? Retreat? Fear? Try to control things or take on their care?
2. What cycles of behavior do you seem triggered by, or fall into, most: anger, resentment, bitterness, hurt, depression? Has anyone ever noticed these patterns of behavior in you and commented on them?
3. What things have you told yourself, encouraging and otherwise, when you've tried to stop cycling in behaviors like controlling or caretaking or spinning into depression?

Chapter 10: Tackling the Trigger Stongholds

1. What would it take for you to confront the person or situation that's triggered your unhealthy behaviors?
2. What therapeutic letter do you need to write? What keeps you from writing it?
3. What change do you pray for by writing a therapeutic letter? What feelings could it release? What difference could it make in your daily life?

Chapter 11: Sweet Surrender

1. In what situations, when you're facing a food trigger, do you most wish someone would fight for you? How have you tried to fight a trigger in the past? What has worked? What didn't?
2. What props have you used to face the enemy of trigger foods, binges, and situations to abuse food? What diets, exercise programs, books, or programs? How long did you stick with each thing and with what results?

3. What does "going another way" look like for you? Describe the differences of your road toward living in recovery as opposed to continuing to live in a cycle of food abuse.
4. What does the "One day at a time" idea do for you? Do you feel released by it or frightened and upset? Why?

Chapter 12: Do What You Can and Let God Do the Rest

1. In your efforts for the week ahead to avoid triggers and eat healthy and well, what things can you do? What things can you not do on your own?
2. For you, what is the most challenging aspect of surrendering things to God? What does surrender mean for you in everyday situations?

Chapter 13: Trigger-Free Eating

1. How many diets have you tried before picking up this book and reading this chapter? What has worked for you and what hasn't? For how long?
2. Think of the statement, "Diets don't work." Do you agree? Why or why not? What is the most surprising thing to you about diets and the idea of exchanges in a food plan?
3. Do you already know your triggers? Does anything surprise you about defining them?

Chapter 14: Developing a Food Plan

1. How many of the alternative names for sugar did you recognize?
2. Have you studied labels before reading this chapter? How often have you put an item back on the shelf and chosen something else because of the ingredient list?
3. Like gum and diet soda, what could possibly be a trigger for you, even if it's a so-called healthy food?

Chapter 15: Eating Out While in Recovery

1. What is the most difficult—eating out or other social situations?

2. Write down your top five difficult situations and how you might get through them with Rhona's advice.
3. How would you handle (or have you handled) the situation where a hostess almost bullies you into trying something you know to be a food trigger for you?

Chapter 16: Build a Winning Support System

1. In the past, where have you looked for support in changing your eating or resisting a trigger? Have you called anyone for support? How did that person help you (or not)?
2. What do you most need from a friend when it comes to support in fighting the urge to overeat or binge? Who would you not call upon for support and why?
3. Would you go to a support group? Why or why not? What would you expect from a group?
4. What are your greatest fears about asking for help from others?
5. How has God been a friend to you? What would you like from friendship with God in overcoming food issues and moving forward in life?
6. How can you surround yourself with support beginning today?

Chapter 17: It's Not Just about the Food

1. In what ways might you shop for food differently now that you're determined to live trigger-free?
2. How can you clean house this week? What foods will you toss?
3. What is the thing you need most to "get" in your recovery from abusing food? Accountability? Encouragement? Know-how and experience? How can you get that thing or those things like you get your daily nutrition? Think of one way for the week ahead, and another way for the week after that.

Rhona Epstein, PsyD, CAC, is a licensed psychologist, certified addictions counselor, and marriage and family therapist in the Philadelphia area. For more than twenty-five years she's led seminars, conferences, and therapeutic workshops, including at the American Association of Christian Counselors World Conference, to help people overcome food addiction and its underlying issues. She received her doctorate in clinical psychology from Chestnut Hill College, and her master's degree in counseling psychology from Temple University. She is passionate, from her own personal experience and recovery from food addiction, about addressing the needs of the whole person (mind, body, and spirit). Learn more at www.MySweetSalvation.com.

WORTHY
PUBLISHING

IF YOU ENJOYED THIS BOOK, WILL YOU CONSIDER
SHARING THE MESSAGE WITH OTHERS?

- Mention the book in a Facebook post, Twitter update,
  Pinterest pin, or blog post.

- Recommend this book to those in your small group, book
  club, workplace, and classes.

- Head over to facebook.com/, "LIKE" the page, and post
  a comment as to what you enjoyed the most.

- Tweet "I recommend reading #FoodTriggers
  by @ RhonaEpstein// @worthypub"

- Pick up a copy for someone you know who would be
  challenged and encouraged by this message.

- Write a book review online.

Visit us at foodtriggersbook.com

You can subscribe to Worthy Publishing's newsletter at
worthypublishing.com.

**WORTHY PUBLISHING
FACEBOOK PAGE**

**WORTHY PUBLISHING
WEBSITE**